The PreTrib Rapture

To My Wife

Fred DeRuvo

www.studygrowknow.com

Published in Scotts Valley, California, by Study-Grow-Know
www.studygrowknow.com • www.adroitpublications.com

Scripture quotations (designated ESB), are from The Holy Bible, English Standard Version®,
copyright © 2001 by Crossway Bibles, a publishing ministry of Good News Publishers. Used
by permission. All rights reserved.

Scripture quoted by permission. Quotations designated (NET) are from the NET Bible® copyright ©1996-2006 by Biblical Studies Press, L.L.C. www.bible.org All rights reserved.

Images used in this publication (unless otherwise noted) are from clipartconnection.com
and used with permission, ©2007 JUPITERIMAGES, and its licensors. All rights reserved.

All Woodcuts used herein are in the Public Domain and free of copyright.

All figure illustrations used in this book were created by the author and protected under
copyright laws, © 2009.

Library of Congress Cataloging-in-Publication Data

DeRuvo, Fred, 1957 –

ISBN 0982644302
EAN-13 9780982644300

1. Religion – Christian Theology – Eschatology

Contents

Foreword

Since 1973, certain individuals have made it their passion and do what they can to *delete* the PreTrib Rapture doctrine from the landscape of the Church. It seems that they have made at least some headway, with their accusations and ire.

However, what is important to note, is not whether they have made gains, but *the way* in which they have made gains. The tactics they use are questionable at best, and the PreTrib Rapture position is wrongly critiqued through the eyes of the particular position they hold.

Many books have been written defending the PreTrib Rapture. This book is a bit different. Instead of defending the PreTrib Rapture doctrine, a serious look is taken of the claims made against the PreTrib Rapture position.

Beyond this, there is an interesting aspect of the entire argument presented against the PreTrib Rapture, which may bring the complete argument into question. ***We are expected to believe a number of things***:

1. Margaret MacDonald created the idea of a PreTrib Rapture based on an alleged vision she had.
2. Edward Irving first preached on the PreTrib Rapture, gaining this knowledge from MacDonald.
3. John Nelson Darby got hold of it, and essentially ran with it, passing it along to C. I. Scofield.
4. From here, as powerful as the Church was at this time in history, so much more powerful were these two individuals that they managed to bamboozle a very large majority of evangelicals within Christendom.
5. This bamboozling including sweeping the table clean of nearly every other then-accepted view of the Rapture or End Times.
6. This was accomplished through the publication of, and forceful "proselytizing" with, the Scofield Study System Bible.
7. Revisionism, plagiarism, and heresy all worked together to create one of the most well planned cover-ups in all the history of the Church!

I could not have come up with a better 'whodunit,' if I had tried. From out of nowhere, MacDonald, Irving, Darby, and then Scofield, all had the same plan, which was to change the course of future history, by rewriting the past, and forcing a new direction. This accusation goes beyond credulity. However, if true, then all that can be said is that these four individuals were more than brilliant. They were by far, the most intelligent individuals that ever walked the face of this earth! The word "genius" does not do them justice. Is this what really occurred? Were these four souls able to work – either individually, or in harmony – to propagate one of the biggest cover-ups the evangelical church has ever known?

This book has been written to respond to at least some of these charges. The major focus of this book though, is to consider the overall charge by those opposed to the PreTrib Rapture position. They assert that a handful of individuals, through the use of revising history and lying, managed to create a tremendous cover-up in the visible Church; a cover-up which has literally pushed aside every other viewpoint with respect to the doctrine of the Rapture of the End Times, so that the PreTrib Rapture position has taken the pole position. I would like to state without equivocation, that while I am of the opinion that the Bible teaches a PreTrib Rapture, and that I am appalled that such charges could be made by intelligent people, I do not consider the doctrine of the Rapture to be the most important doctrine in all of Christendom.

At least some of the reasons why I believe the PreTrib Rapture to be taught in Scripture will be explained. However, I would also like to clearly and unabashedly point out, in the strongest terms possible, that it really does not matter to me. What is meant by that is that while I view the physical return of the Lord Jesus Christ as the climax in the history of this world, I do not dwell on this, to the exclusion of all other subjects that the Bible teaches. Some have made it their career to espouse a particular viewpoint related to the Rapture, or the End Times in general. I believe a proper mindset regarding the End Times, prompts (all) Christians to expect His return, and be *purified* in thought, word and deed because of it. Those who forget that He is coming back, wind up becoming like the lazy servants, who had forgotten the master of the house would return one day. During his absence, they began to mistreat the rest in the household (cf. Mark 13:34-37). So, the extremes become apparent. On one hand, we have the individual who only speaks about the End Times, over-emphasizing it, and on the other hand, the individual who never speaks of it, forgetting its importance.

As we think about the climax of future world history, the return of the Lord and the eventual Eternal Order, which will follow, we *should* become focused on everything that brings glory to God in Christ. Too often, however, we fail at this point. We run around discussing and looking for all the signs, which we believe, point to His return, yet we do not exhibit the same concern for the lost. We want to know what heaven will be like, and while there is nothing wrong with that, if it becomes our primary focus, we could very easily become as someone has said, so heavenly minded, that we are essentially no earthly good.

Discussing aspects of the End Times, along with other doctrines of the Bible is a godly pursuit. Nevertheless, it should always be tempered with the question, '*How does this study and my learning from it glorify the Lord?* 'If we are unsure how to answer that question, then chances are we have gone off on a tangent, as many have done and continue to do today. Ultimately, disagreements over aspects of the End Times should always be done with reverence for Christ and love of the saints. This is not true. To some, because I believe in a PreTrib Rapture, I am considered a heretic, someone who is in serious danger of losing salvation. Because of my PreTrib Rapture belief, I am guilty of deceiving people. As one individual wrote in an email not long ago, "*The bottom line is that you promote a false doctrine. It was organized into the form it is today, and thus originated with J.N. Darby. Simple implications of PTR by a few people (not many, as you exaggerated [sic]) does not a organized doctrine make not a eschatological precedent set, as any reasonable individual understands and agrees with. PTR is a breeding ground for apathy, complacency, and sets people up for entrance into the Great Apostasy. It is one of the deadly doctrines that will doom millions of people to eternal damnation. That is not to say that all who believe PTR will be so deceived. I know Christians that believe false doctrines who are sincerely devoted to God. God will judge all of us in that regard when the time comes. However, God will judge more harshly those who promote false doc-*

trine at the last judgment (you should know the scripture reference for this fact).[1] (emphasis added)

Note the severity of this individual's judgment. The PreTrib Rapture doctrine is apparently so heinous, that it will "doom millions of people to eternal damnation." This individual also rejects eternal security, believing instead that salvation can be lost. It boggles the mind to see how people can be so quick to judge and to judge with the type of dogmatism that is expressed in the above email. This is tragic. Nowhere (that I am aware of), in Scripture is it implied or stated that confusion or even a deliberate misunderstanding of doctrines related to the End Times is cause for banishment to eternal punishment. However, this person so believes that nearly all who espouse the PreTrib Rapture doctrine are not only deceived, but deceive others and because of it, their "reward" is to be cast into hell. He has elevated this particular doctrine to the level of the nature of God, the deity of Christ, the Trinity, etc. Study of the End Times is just that – *study*. There is a certain amount of ambiguity in Scripture, which is at least one of the reasons a variety of opinions prevail on the subject. However, it must be asked, '*Why is it that only the PreTrib Rapture position is the one that is held out to the possibility of eternal condemnation and no other?*' We will do our best to respond to that within these pages.

I enjoy studying and thinking about spending eternity with Christ. I often think of being reunited with my sister, who has gone on ahead of me. I grow weary of realizing my own sinfulness and though all of my sin is forgiven and forgotten by God, my sin nature remains and with that, the promise of sinning in the future.

I spend much more time simply studying Scripture and dealing with topics that are useful for me daily. Like Paul, I want to know Christ and the power of His resurrection. Though I am told in Ephesians 2, that I am already seated with Christ in the heavenlies, I still want to please my Lord and Savior *now*, while I live within my earthly tent. I do not (nor will I), live in sinless perfection. Unfortunately, I will sin from time to time as I continue to walk through this life, until Christ calls me home. My goal is to be like Him,

---

[1] Email received dated 07/11/2009 at 8:44am from C. H. Fisher (on file)

and I know that occurs only as I draw close to Him, through prayer and the study of His Word.

Study of the End Times is rewarding, as it causes me to study more of the Old Testament than I might normally study. It encourages me that one day, I will be with Him, and I will bow before Him, casting any crowns He will have given me, at His feet. I know that as John says, when we see Him, we will be like Him (cf. 1 John 3:2-3). That, my brothers and sisters, is the goal that should motivate every single Christian. It changes the way I live today and creates a heart of compassion for the lost.

- Fred DeRuvo – September 2009

Chapter 1
Birds of a Feather Naysay Together

P robably the number one claim that Posttribulation Rapturists make against the PreTrib Rapture position, is that this position tends to promote:

- *Complacency*
- *Spiritual immaturity*
- *Lack of preparedness of persecution*
- *Less likely to encourage evangelism*

The above reasons are fabricated. In other words, those who attempt to refute the PreTrib Rapture position, do so by providing artificial reasons for what they feel is its lack of veracity. Are they correct? Do they have a leg to stand on?

Most Posttribulationalists, without hesitation, will inform all that the early Church was Posttribulationalist in viewpoint, as stated. It is rare to find a Posttribulationalist, who does not believe that the early Church was not Posttribulational in viewpoint, with respect to the Rapture.

Then to hear and understand their argument, one would think that looking at the early Church – as Posttribulationalist in Rapture position – meant that they were the exact *opposite* of the bulleted list above. In other words, since the charge is made that one who adopts a PreTrib Rapture position would result in the above bulleted points, then it stands to reason that those who believe and espouse a Posttribulational Rapture position, would:

- *Be alert*
- *Be spiritually mature*
- *Be prepared for coming persecution*
- *Be much more likely to evangelize*

To determine whether this is true, then all we need to do is look through the New Testament to determine exactly what these allegedly Posttribulational Rapture Christians were actually like. Since there is much in the New Testament, specifically with Paul's epistles, then this is most definitely not something that it is at all difficult to ascertain.

The first place we can begin is with Paul's letter to the Corinthian believers. This was a congregation of believers in the early Church, founded by Paul. They had been under his teaching for some time, and he had obviously put a great deal of work into bringing them to

Christ, and helping them to refine their lives. What then was the reason Paul wrote to the Corinthians?

Carnal

The Corinthian believers were carnal. There were divisions because of this carnal attitude and outlook. Paul states, "*I urge you, brothers and sisters, by the name of our Lord Jesus Christ, to agree together, to end your divisions, and to be united by the same mind and purpose. For members of Chloe's household have made it clear to me, my brothers and sisters, that there are quarrels among you,*" (1 Corinthians 1:10-11; NET). He goes on to explain what those quarrels were, by telling them that it is wrong to be "followers of Paul," or "followers of Apollos."

Paul ends this rebuke with a powerful question, "*Is Christ divided? Paul wasn't crucified for you, was he? Or were you, in fact, baptized in the name of Paul?*" (v. 13 NET). Like little babies, the Corinthians believers were boasting about the fact that some were baptized by Paul, while some were baptized by Apollos. This division-causing arrogance should not have been.

Paul then explains to them that it is the message of the cross that is important, not who baptizes whom. Any boasting, should be boasting in what Jesus Christ has accomplished on behalf of the Christian.

Paul then tries to help them understand (beginning in chapter 2), that their true calling is found in the permanence of their heavenly position. It is from this position that true spirituality comes to the believer.

In 1 Corinthians 3, Paul harshly (yet lovingly), expresses his frustration with them because he was unable to speak to them as mature Christians. They were still spiritual infants. As he points out in chapter 4, it was Paul's desire to correct them as a loving father corrects his wayward son.

Chapter 5 begins a discussion on church discipline and the need for it. It was especially applicable to this church because of the sin that seemed so prevalent within its body. A son has his father's wife and the believers in Corinth are proud of it! Not only that, but also some believers were taking other believers to court! As Paul says, *this should not be!*

Paul then exhorts them on celibacy, marriage, and even remaining single. Why? Because of the times they lived in and the mounting persecution, "*Because of the impending crisis I think it best for you to remain as you are,*" (7:26; NET).

He then has to deal with eating food, which had been sacrificed to idols, in chapter 8. Apparently, there was a type of legalism that some were forcing on others. Paul straightened the situation out for them.

The entirety of Paul's first epistle to the Corinthian believers is filled with exhortation, rebuke, and a reminder that they were not as spiritual as they apparently thought they were which necessitated his correction.

Nevertheless, what happened here? If the early church was Posttribulational in Rapture position, *why* is there evidence of extreme spiritual immaturity, which obviously existed? In fact, the circumstances were such that the persecution was real, palpable and *at the door*! They should have been casting their cares on Jesus, but instead were filled with jealously, carnality, and spiritual immaturity!

They were completely unprepared for the coming persecution. To hear the Posttribulationalist tell it, these early Christians were most definitely *not expecting* the Rapture to occur before the Tribulation/Great Tribulation.

Knowing this then, we must ask how the assertions from Posttribulationalists and others that the early Church did not expect to be rescued from the coming Tribulation/Great Tribulation by any Rapture, impact the argument that adopting a PreTrib Rapture position creates spiritually immature Christians?

Ladies and Gentlemen, the Enigmatic Dave MacPherson!

Without giving him too much credit, it is generally recognized by his groupies and followers, that Dave MacPherson is the *go-to* person on all things set against the Pretribulation Rapture position. Known also known as the PreTrib Rapture, which is the belief that prior to the Tribulation/Great Tribulation period of seven years, Christ will call His Bride home to be with Him, without His Bride experiencing death, this based on 2 Thessalonians).

In 1973, his first book on the subject was published titled, *The Unbelievable Pre-Trib Origin: the Recent Discovery of a Well-Known Theory's Beginning and Its Incredible Cover-Up*. From that point, no less than seven additional books were published on the same subject.

Obviously, arguing against the PreTrib Rapture position has been good for Dave MacPherson. Noted by many as a true scholar and journalist, he unfortunately brings to the entire issue of the PreTrib Rapture, a good amount of baggage, for the lack of a better word.

Dave's Dad a Posttributulationist

Dave's father, Dr. Norman Spurgeon Macpherson, was a Baptist Minister, and, it should be noted, was a Posttributulationist. He published a number of books such as *Triumph Through Tribulation*, *Tell It Like It Will Be*, as well as other books and articles. The first book mentioned, contains twenty arguments against the PreTrib Rapture position, in which Dr. MacPherson takes the time to rebut each of them.

In short, Posttributulationism is a belief that the Church will experience the Tribulation/Great Tribulation. There will be no Rapture prior or during any part of this seven-year period. Furthermore, part of this belief is the idea that the Church should not shrink from persecution, or trials or any tribulation at all. In fact, for many, the Church needs to be purified and should the Tribulation/Great Tribulation occur sooner, or later, whatever generation of the Church is alive to experience that terrible time, she should go through it willingly, grateful for the opportunity to suffer for our Savior, as He suffered for us.

Another important point is often found in the Posttribulationist's definition of "church." For them, in spite of Paul's point that he alone revealed the mystery of the Church, Posttribulationists claim that the "church" *is* found in the Old Testament. They point to the usage of the word *ekklesia*, as used in numerous OT passages, which they say proves the presence of the Church. Since the Church was present in the Old Testament (according to them), then when words like "saints" are used in Revelation, it alludes to the presence of the Church. It should be noted though, that after Revelation chapter three, the word "church" does not appear.

Posttribulationalists also view the doctrine of *imminency* differently than those who support a PreTrib Rapture position. Imminency is the concept that Christ could return at any moment, because there is nothing, which precludes it. This imminency of course, as with anything else, must be understood in light of Scripture. If Christ is saying that He could literally come back at any moment, is He referring to His Second Coming? Is He referring to the PreTrib Rapture? Is He referring to something else altogether? We will spend a bit of time answering these questions.

Like Father, Like Son
Growing up in a household in which this belief was held, it is natural to understand that his son Dave, would eventually grow to adulthood and adopt the same set of beliefs as his father. Though Dave Mac-Pherson is probably one of the more well known of the two, it was Dr. Norman MacPherson who wrote on the subject first. He took the position against the PreTrib Rapture, long before his son ventured into that arena.

Dave MacPherson has made a name for himself by writing about one subject, and one subject only: the PreTrib Rapture. It is almost as if Dave has nothing else to say, so intent is he on eradicating a belief that he strongly believes is errant. We will certainly delve more deeply into this entire area, but for now, simply mentioning it will suffice.

Other Writers

Since 1973, and the publication of Dave MacPherson's first book, things have taken off for those who stand against the PreTrib Rapture position. Many books have been written on the subject and the PreTrib Rapture position has been called everything from simply *wrong*, to *heretical,* to *the End Times deception*, and everything in between.

One would almost think that for as often as PreTrib Rapturists are accused of making a ton of money from the proceeds of book sales, movies and the rest, it appears as though those who stand against the PreTrib Rapture are not doing so bad either.

Many individuals portray the PreTrib Rapture as something that is abhorrent. Brian M. Schwertley states this, regarding the PreTrib Rapture position, *"Whenever a Christian encounters a doctrine that has not been taught by anyone in any branch of Christ's church for over eighteen centuries, one should be very suspect of that teaching. This fact, in and of itself, does not prove that the new teaching is false."*[2]

By that reasoning then, we are forced to reject Calvin's doctrinal stances, as well as Luther's, based on their newness, a scant 200 years prior to Darby. In fact, it would appear that the doctrine of salvation solely by grace is suspect, since it was not until the Reformation that the absence of it was highlighted by Luther, et al.

---

[2] http://www.reformedonline.com/view/reformedonline/rapture.htm

In truth, it would appear that aside from Premillennialism, Amillennialism might be the second oldest doctrinal position. Premillennialism is the belief that Christ will physically return to earth *prior* to His Millennial reign. He will then set up His kingdom here on earth and reign for 1,000 years. Amillennialism is the belief that there will be *no* future, literal, 1,000-year reign of Christ on this earth.

Regarding Amillennialism, Walvoord comments, "*It is significant that the first successful opposition to premillennialism came from the adoption of a spiritualizing principle of interpretation. The Alexandrian school of theology which came into prominence about 300 A.D. followed a principle of interpretation, which regarded all Scripture as an allegory. They succeeded in arousing a considerable opposition to premillenarians of their day even if it was at the price of subverting not only the millennial doctrine but all other Christian doctrine as well. It remained for Augustine to give a more moderate application of this principle of interpretation. In general, he held that only prophecy should be spiritualized and that in the historical and doctrinal sections of Scripture the 'historical-grammatical' literal method should be used. This was a decided improvement as far as theology as a whole was concerned, even if it left the millennial issue unsolved and at the mercy of the allegorical school. Because of the weight of Augustine in other major issues of theology where he was in the main correct, Augustine became the model for the Protestant Reformers, who accepted his amillennialism along with his other teachings.*"[3] Just because something is "old" historically, that, in and of itself, does not prove its genuineness. Maybe Mr. Schwertley is Amillennial himself, so he would have no difficulty with this.

Good Ol' Margaret...Again
Others provide a different outlook on the PreTrib Rapture position. Marv Rosenthal, himself an avowed PreTrib Rapturist for years, prior

---

[3] http://bible.org/seriespage/millennial-series-part-5-amillennialism-method-interpretation

to embracing the Pre-Wrath Rapture position, stated, *"To thwart the Lord's warning to His children, in 1830, ' proclaims Rosenthal, 'Satan, the 'father of lies,' gave to a fifteen-year-old girl named Margaret MacDonald a lengthy vision'."*[4] Apparently, Rosenthal earnestly believes he was completely deceived by Satan himself before he adopted the Pre-Wrath Rapture position.

As with Rosenthal, most folks lay out their complaints against the PreTrib Rapture position by referencing church history. Others, like R. A. Taylor, put forth arguments that reference Scripture, making sweeping generalizations like, *"It contradicts the plain teaching of scripture. The Second Coming, the rapture, and the resurrection of the dead occur at the same time, on the last day. 1 Th 4:14 -18, John 6:39 ff.*[5] But this person's belief, is in opposition to Rosenthal's Pre-Wrath position. Please note also, that Taylor presents his opinions as fact. Obviously, others would (and have), disagree with him over his un-

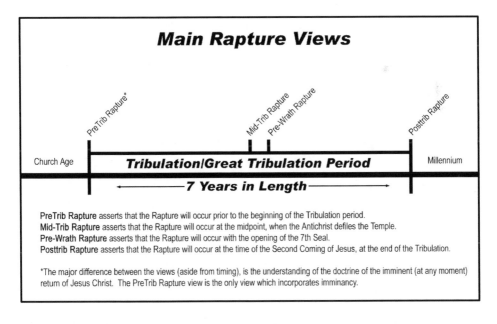

Main Rapture Views

PreTrib Rapture* Mid-Trib Rapture Pre-Wrath Rapture Posttrib Rapture

Church Age | **Tribulation/Great Tribulation Period** | Millennium

← **7 Years in Length** →

PreTrib Rapture asserts that the Rapture will occur prior to the beginning of the Tribulation period.
Mid-Trib Rapture asserts that the Rapture will occur at the midpoint, when the Antichrist defiles the Temple.
Pre-Wrath Rapture asserts that the Rapture will occur with the opening of the 7th Seal.
Posttrib Rapture asserts that the Rapture will occur at the time of the Second Coming of Jesus, at the end of the Tribulation.

*The major difference between the views (aside from timing), is the understanding of the doctrine of the imminent (at any moment) return of Jesus Christ. The PreTrib Rapture view is the only view which incorporates imminancy.

---

[4] Marvin J. Rosenthal, "Is the Church in Matthew Chapter 24?" *Zion's Fire* (Nov-Dec 1994), p. 10
[5] http://www.apocalipsis.org/rap-rebut.htm

derstanding of the "plain teaching of scripture." It would appear that Taylor has not allowed Scripture to interpret itself (with respect to the End Times); explaining how these future events will play out. It is not as if the whole of the Bible or even the whole of the New Testament was brought to bear on the 1 Thessalonians 4:14-18, John 6:39 (and following), passages to which he refers.

If we look at just these two passages of Scripture carefully, it should become clear that they do not even necessarily relate to the *same* event spoken of by Paul and Christ:

"For if we believe that Jesus died and rose again, so also we believe that God will bring with him those who have fallen asleep as Christians. For we tell you this by the word of the Lord, that we who are alive, who are left until the coming of the Lord, will surely not go ahead of those who have fallen asleep. For the Lord himself will come down from heaven with a shout of command, with the voice of the archangel and with the trumpet of God, and the dead in Christ will rise first. Then we who are alive, who are left, will be suddenly caught up together with them in the clouds to meet the Lord in the air. And so we will always be with the Lord. Therefore encourage one another with these words," (1 Thessalonians 4:14-18).

"Now this is the will of the one who sent me – that I should not lose one person of every one he has given me, but raise them all up at the last day," (John 6:39).

Notice how Taylor's opinions are presented *dogmatically as fact.* Taylor apparently believes that since there *appears* to be a lack of time between the events, then they all occur together. Does Scripture itself bear this out?

If we were to follow that rule, then we must apply the same logic to passages like Zechariah 9:9-10, which reads:

*"**9** Rejoice greatly, O daughter of Zion!*

Shout aloud, O daughter of Jerusalem!

Behold, your king is coming to you;

righteous and having salvation is he,

humble and mounted on a donkey,

on a colt, the foal of a donkey.

10 *I will cut off the chariot from Ephraim*

and the war horse from Jerusalem;

and the battle bow shall be cut off,

and he shall speak peace to the nations;

his rule shall be from sea to sea,

and from the River to the ends of the earth."

It should be obvious that verse nine highlights Jesus' *first advent*, while verse ten highlights His *second advent*. There is absolutely no *space of time* evidenced between the two events. Taylor would also be forced to apply the same understanding to these two verses, by rejecting the idea that any space of time between the two advents is implied, since none is seen in the verses themselves. Of course, we know that this is not true and other portions of Scripture verify this for us. Beyond this, we know from history that Jesus already came to this planet, and we await His Second Coming, so there must be a time lapse between the two verses.

The PreTrib Rapture and Christian Martyrdom

Taylor presents the following as a rebuttal to the PreTrib Rapture doctrine; "*The idea that the church will not go through the great tribulation ignores those Christians who have been martyred down through the ages and those Christians now undergoing persecution throughout*

the world. It is a doctrine that could only survive in an environment
where the church is not currently undergoing persecution."[6]

However, this in and of itself, is not a viable (or even accurate), reason at all. It is difficult to know how the PreTrib Rapture position ignores those Christians who have been martyred through the ages, especially, when it still occurs. Taylor seems to be the one who is ignoring the fact that even in modern times, Christians are routinely killed in various parts of the world, and they are specifically killed because of their faith in Christ. Even on our home soil, people have been killed because of their faith in Christ, as tragic events such as two students taking over a school and killing a number of fellow students at Columbine shows.

While it is often difficult to obtain accurate numbers, the fact remains that many Christians are routinely killed, solely because they are Christians. What existed during the time of the early Church has sprung to life again in these latter days.

International *Christian Concern's Hall of Shame Report 2009*[7], presents information on the ten worst persecuting nations of Christians today. They are (in the order in which they were listed):

1. *North Korea*
2. *Iraq*
3. *Saudi Arabia*
4. *Somalia*
5. *India*
6. *China*
7. *Pakistan*
8. *Iran*
9. *Eritrea*
10. *Vietnam*

---

[6] http://www.apocalipsis.org/rap-rebut.htm
[7] http://persecution.org/suffering/pdfs/ICC_Hall_of_Shame_2009.pdf

Each of the above listed countries is rated by the International Christian Concern, for its *scope, intensity,* and *trend* in persecuting Christians. From the end of 2007, through the middle of 2008, there were a total of 16 deaths, and 10 arrests.

Iraq has many more to their shame. From January 2008 until November 2008, there were:

- *31 murders*
- *219 murders by bombing (of churches, or Christian gatherings)*
- *1 known torture of a priest*
- *1 rape*
- *Over 3,000 death threats*

Saudi Arabia has *deported 15,* and *murdered 1 Christian.*

In Somalia, one man was killed by three cousins because he stated he was a Christian. Another man, refusing to pray toward Mecca because he had become a Christian, was summarily executed by two Muslims. Beyond this, *9 others were murdered for their faith,* and *20 others were beaten, kidnapped, raped, or imprisoned for their faith.* A number of the beatings took place as the church, the individuals were pulled from, was being demolished.

In India, in 2008, the same organization has an extensive report of the vast amount of Christians, who gave up their lives for their faith. The report contains 39 pages of crimes against Christians, containing *267 murders* alone. Beyond this, there were hundreds of *death threats, tortures, rapes, kidnappings, arrests, legal discriminations, vandalism, forcible conversion, a halt to worship, property destruction, false charges and accusations, arson and harassment.*

China also included many pages of crimes against Christians. Russia and others are not even fully known to us. Do we need to continue? It is obvious that there is no lack of martyrdom, as well as the "lesser" crimes being perpetrated against Christians throughout the world. Because it is not necessarily experienced in the United States...yet, this does not mean it does not occur.

Jesus Promises Tribulation

There is no guarantee from Jesus or anywhere else in the Bible, that Christians will *not* experience tribulations and trials. In fact, Jesus promised that we *would* experience them (cf. John 16:33). What many do not seem to distinguish though, is the difference between *normal* (if you can call it that), or general persecutions and tribulations, and the *wrath of God* that is going to be poured out during the entirety of the Tribulation/Great Tribulation. From the very first seal that is opened, it is apparent that God is fully in control because He is the One who commands them to be opened. His wrath is associated with each seal, trumpet, and bowl. He oversees the entire period of the Tribulation/Great Tribulation.

The PreTrib Rapture doctrine does *not* ignore the martyrdom of multitudes of Christians down through the centuries. It also does not deny that persecutions and tribulations are occurring *now* in various parts of the world. However, the Tribulation/Great Tribulation, as disclosed by Jesus Himself in the Olivet Discourse (cf. Matthew 24, Mark 13 and Luke 21), is said to be *the* worst tribulation the world will ever have seen. In other words, this particular brand of tribulation is unlike the tribulations that Christians often experience in this world. Since this particular Tribulation/Great Tribulation is due to the fact that God's wrath is being poured out onto the world, how can it be justified that Christians need to experience God's wrath, when in point of fact, we have already been *saved from it?*

The "Special" Church of the West

"If the pre-trib rapture doctrine is false then it means that many Christians will be unprepared for tribulation and persecution when it comes upon them. What makes the church in the West so special that it will

24

not undergo persecution?"[8] This is another assumption on the part of the individual making the statement. *Nothing* makes the church in the west special. However, it is obvious that persecution comes in many forms. When dealing with direct persecution based on one's *beliefs*, it is almost easier, in some ways, to stand against it, by remaining firm in the faith. If someone put a gun to a Christian's head and stated, *"Curse Jesus Christ, or die,"* it would be relatively *easy for an authentic Christian* to make that decision, wouldn't it? The idea that in one split second, death will usher the Christian into paradise, is hardly something from which the genuine Christian would shy away.

However, here in the western world, Christians daily deal with all kinds of problems and difficulties that are often *more* damaging to the soul than having to die for the faith, due to their insidious nature. We are continually bombarded with prurient advertising, TV shows, music and movies, whether we want to be or not. It is impossible to go on the Internet without seeing unwanted "pop-up" ads literally popping up questionable material. The decisions that Christians in the western world face, while not as obvious as possibly losing one's life because of our faith, we are, nonetheless, faced with having to make decisions with respect to our faith on a day-by-day basis.

The Difficulty of Being Christian in the Western World
I would suggest that it is often more difficult to be a Christian in a pluralistic society like America, where our rights as Americans are being eroded or directly removed continually. While it is not yet stated that being a Christian is a crime punishable by death, it is becoming clearer that being a Christian in today's western society is not a position to be admired. Television shows, movies, music, news articles, books and more, all ridicule the Christian. We are called hate-mongers for simply stating that homosexuality is wrong. Many Christians, who own businesses throughout California, have reported

---

[8] http://www.apocalipsis.org/rap-rebut.htm

being boycotted when it is learned that they voted against Proposition 8. In various parts of the United States, it has become against the law to offer prayers at certain events; events, in which prayer was publicly offered for decades with no question.

Within the fabric of the western society, the attack on Christians and Christianity has become extremely insidious, that it is almost not noticed by the average person. This makes it even more difficult to take a stand at times because of the unfavorable attitude that results from doing so, by those outside the Church.

If faced with the decision to recant Jesus, or die for Him, all authentic Christians would die for Him. Yet, in America, the testing of our faith, the temptations we face, and the trials that come upon us are completely different in form and content. Being much more subtle in appearance, Christians are often unaware of their presence until it is too late.

Complacency

"[The PreTrib Rapture] fosters complacency within the church and in the world. It gives those left behind a second chance and is less likely to encourage evangelism and missionary efforts because the great commission will be fulfilled by the 144,000 and the two witnesses rather than the church. The job of the Great Commission belongs to the Church."[9] This is another example of an assumption by Taylor.

It is difficult to know how believing that Jesus will step out of the third heaven to call His Bride home, fosters complacency. While it might do this in people who do not take their Christianity seriously to begin with, in general, as we read in the first epistle of John, the hope of His return purifies us; *"Beloved, we are God's children now, and what we will be has not yet appeared; but we know that when he appears we shall be like him, because we shall see him as he is. And*

---

[9] http://www.apocalipsis.org/rap-rebut.htm

everyone who thus hopes in him purifies himself as he is pure," (1 John 3:2-3).

In other words, what John is saying is that as we consider the *fact* of Christ's return, we are motivated to live lives that please Him. We will see the things that are worthy and those which are unworthy because we will be comparing our actions and our thoughts to Christ. If He were to come today, physically sitting right next to us, would we be embarrassed by some of the things that we do, think or say?

Thinking about the fact that Jesus is going to return, puts our minds where they belong; on our heavenly dwelling when we will see Jesus in person. It is when we do *not* contemplate our union with Christ, and the fact that we will one day speak with Him *face to face,* that we tend to drift from the faith.

Dad Returns Home
When I was a young boy during the summer, my dad would often leave the house in the morning for work, but before doing so, he might have instructions for me related to jobs that I was to take care of before he returned home. Invariably, I would spend most of the day playing with friends. We would literally lose ourselves playing tag, touch or tackle football, or go riding on our bikes exploring unknown areas of the country we had not seen before.

Playtime would continue and if I did remember my dad's instructions to me, I would generally tell myself something like *"There will be time to get the jobs done before Dad comes home."* Telling myself this, always gave me more reason to continue playing. However, as the day wore on and the jobs were still not done, I began to consider the ramifications of my dad's return home and the status of the jobs I was supposed to have done.

This would normally put me in a bit of a bind because I then realized that I did not have time to finish the jobs done before my father returned. I would try my best to enlist the help of a friend, but all too often, they needed to be home themselves.

On one occasion, I remember weeding the garden area by the front door...*in the dark!* I started about fifteen minutes before my dad came home and was not even close to being done. As Dad's car pulled up, my heart raced. He got out, walked toward the door, and we greeted one another, as I worked feverishly to show that I was doing my best.

Later, after dinner, my dad asked me about my day. He simply asked what I had done. Starting to relax, I told him. After explaining what I had done all day, he looked at me and asked, *"Then you had enough time to get the jobs done, right?"* Gulp. I had to admit that I would have had enough time. He looked at me and simply said, *"Okay. Enough said."*

Now, had I spent the entire day honestly concerned about getting those jobs done, I would likely have done them much earlier, even prior to playing with my friends. I would have gotten them done, and had more time to play and relax without worry. I could have even played longer. When I returned home, instead of feverishly trying to complete the jobs, I would have walked into the house, and possibly enjoyed some TV time (the shows were good then). When my father returned home for the day, I would have waited expectantly for him to compliment me on the work I had done and everything would have been hunky dory. That was not the case, though.

However, isn't this the point of the parable of the lazy servants? Here are people who literally stopped thinking about the fact that the master of the house would return. Because they stopped thinking about it, they become slothful, evil, abusive, and arrogant. Had they continued to ponder the master's return, they would not have acted that way, but instead would have continued taking care of the master's household. They would have remembered that he was going to return, and they would have wanted the household to be in tiptop shape upon his arrival back home.

Reflecting on His Return Should Keep Us Alert

Actually, far from causing people to become complacent, or lazy, I believe that the proper understanding of the Lord's any moment return, becomes the catalyst for right living. It should cause us to remember that we are on this earth to *complete* His business. If we forget that He is going to return and take us off the planet, then *that* is the reason, according to Scripture, we will grow complacent, and lazy.

In fact, Peter indirectly refers to this when he states that in the Last Days, there will be scoffers who wonder aloud, "*knowing this first of all, that scoffers will come in the last days with scoffing, following their own sinful desires. They will say, "Where is the promise of his coming? For ever since the fathers fell asleep, all things are continuing as they were from the beginning of creation,*" (2 Peter 3:3-4). Peter then states that what may appear to be slowness on God's part is really a sign of His love and patience, since He does not want anyone to perish.

Peter then explains that, "*But the day of the Lord will come like a thief, and then the heavens will pass away with a roar, and the heavenly bodies will be burned up and dissolved, and the earth and the works that are done on it will be exposed,*" (2 Peter 3:10).

The times are in God's hands, and His return will be like a thief to those who are unprepared. All of this leads Peter to ask a question regarding the type of lives Christians should live here on earth. He states, "*Since all these things are thus to be dissolved, what sort of people ought you to be in lives of holiness and godliness, waiting for and hastening the coming of the day of God, because of which the heavens will be set on fire and dissolved, and the heavenly bodies will melt as they burn! However, according to his promise we are waiting for new heavens and a new earth in which righteousness dwells,"* (2 Peter 3:11-13).

Peter clearly states that *"we are **waiting** for new heavens and a new earth,"* and it is equally clear that the implication is to *think* about those things. Our reward for living this life as Christians is eternal life in Christ, to be lived out with Him and all the saints, with new heavens and a new earth. Surely, this is something we should seriously consider.

Another rebuttal is stated like this; *"[The PreTrib Rapture] gives a false interpretation of the place of the church and Israel within the bible [sic] especially in the interpretation of the book of Revelation. Revelation is interpreted more from the point of view of Israel than the church (to whom it was written in the first place) see Rev 1:4, 22:16.*[10]

I hate to be repetitive. However, it is clear that the above is simply another assumption, and a bad one at that. What the individual fails to realize when he makes the comment *"to whom it was written in the first place,"* is that what John has largely done in Revelation (under the direction of Christ), is to compile many Old Testament passages, placing them all under one heading; that of *Revelation*. Though John wrote the book for the Church, it does not automatically indicate that the contents of the book are directly *for* the Church, but essentially for the Church's *knowledge*.

Dogmatic Is as Dogmatic Does
He also dogmatically states that the PreTrib Rapture position falsely interprets the place of the Church and Israel in the Bible. The trouble is that others would come along and offer statements in rebuttal to his, that are just as dogmatic, which serves no purpose. It all boils down to *how* these things are viewed in Scripture. For instance, many see the Church as having replaced Israel. Since they believe

---

[10] http://www.apocalipsis.org/rap-rebut.htm

that the Church is now the "new" Israel, then when John speaks to Israel in Revelation, he is actually speaking to the "new" Israel, or the Church. It all depends upon how one *gets* to that point, which makes the difference between seeing a difference between Israel and the Church, or not.

A final quote for this chapter is this one; "*Because this doctrine is a modern one invented by men (1830). It is not supported by the church fathers or any of the major creeds or confessions - The Apostles Creed, the Nicene Creed, the Westminster Confession of Faith etc. It is hardly the faith that was once for all entrusted to the saints.*"[11]

Again, what has been stated is not supportable (that the PreTrib Rapture is a modern invention). In fact, it has been shown that references to the PreTrib Rapture go back to the Pseudo-Ephrem document and possibly before. This particular document is dated from the 7th century or earlier (as early as the 3rd). Scholars will continue to debate the date, and content. This is no different from what critics have been doing regarding the Bible for centuries. Readers are encouraged to decide for themselves what the document actually states.

If we look closely at church history, we will see that there were many disagreements between church fathers, some of whom were direct disciples of the original apostles. It is not as if the early church was devoid of error. We know that Paul dealt with error on numerous occasions, in Galatians and Corinthians, as examples, and he of course, was still alive. The error could not even wait until he had passed onto the Lord!

The church fathers, while a secondary source of theology (with the apostles being a primary source, after Christ Himself), did not *write* Scripture. They wrote books about what they knew, and what they

---

[11] http://www.apocalipsis.org/rap-rebut.htm

were taught. None of their works should be confused with the inspired books and epistles of the Bible. While we can look to them to get a feel for the types of disagreements, which existed during their lives, we cannot look to them to settle theological disputes.

Isn't That a Double Standard?

In fact, those who opposed the PreTrib Rapture position are often the first to go outside the Bible in their attempts to discredit the doctrine. However, we see a double standard at work. When the PreTrib Rapturist goes outside the Bible for evidence, those opposed are quick to claim that the words of these individuals are being taken out of context. They might also charge that the individual quoted was never really a PreTrib Rapturist to begin with, even if they *did* write about it.

So on one hand, those opposed to the PreTrib Rapture position, will go *outside* the Bible when it seems to support their conclusions. However, when those in support of the PreTrib Rapture position do the same, an attack is made on the source of the quote(s).

Protesting Too Much?

Like Anti-Zionism though, one has to wonder why there is so much rancor related to the subject of the PreTrib Rapture. Why are people simply unable to discuss it *without* becoming overheated? Why does the subject of the PreTrib Rapture cause such sharp reaction by those who disagree with it? Certainly, these are valuable questions. It is almost as if some of those who stand opposed to the PreTrib Rapture, are protesting a bit *too* much.

The real tragedy is that none of their posturing is pleasing to the Lord, yet they turn, facing the PreTrib Rapturist, saying, clearly, that we are destined to hell. Listen to the tone of this email received directly from Tim Warner. We had sent an email, asking for his opinion on the testimony of people like the Shepherd of Hermas, Victorinus, Jerome, Reverend Dolcino, Joseph Mede, Increase Mather, John

Asgill, Philip Doddridge, John Gill, Morgan Edwards, and Thomas Scott, all of whom came *prior* to J. N. Darby.

Our email to him simply stated, *"Hi Tim, When you get some time, would you mind commenting on this information listed below? I would appreciate it and would enjoy knowing your "take" on it. Regards, Fred."*

Mr. Warner's response is as follows (leaving nothing out): *"I have already dealt with the first two quotes, (from the Shepherd of Hermas and Victorinus), in my article titled, "Pretribulationist Revisionism" [link omitted - author]. In that article I exposed the **blatant lies** of pretribulationist authors, who misquote ancient authors out of context in an attempt to make pretribulationists out of them. Take a look at that article. It tells the truth.*

*A perfect example of these **blatant lies** are the claims that when someone used the word "rapture" that must make them a pretribulationist. Hogwash! I use the word "rapture" too, and I am no pretribulationist. I would wager that most in that list are the same kind of revisionism.*

*Instead of making **bold claims** about the eschatology of these men, why doesn't Thomas Ice actually provide extensive quotations of them, so their words can be judged fairly in context? They won't do this, because they are well aware that **their lies** would be exposed. Providing two or three sentences means nothing. I have seen all too often how they spin excerpts, omit words and phrases, etc, in an attempt to portray men as pretribulationists, when they were nothing of the kind. Pseudo-Ephraim, who was claimed by Jeffrey and Ice as a pretribulationist, is another example of this kind of deception.*

Belief in "imminence" is often claimed to be proof of pretribulationism. Nonsense! Almost all the Reformation era believers held to "historicism," the belief that the "tribulation" covers 1260 years (from the rise of the Roman Catholic Church to the second coming). They held that the Antichrist is the Roman Church and papacy. Many "historicists" believed that the "rapture" was imminent, because they thought the tribulation was about over. Their imminence had NOTHING to do with a "pretribulation rapture."

Why do Thomas Ice, Jeffrey, and other pretribbers only make these kinds of bold claims, yet fail to actually produce the documents in question, so they can be examined? Tim"[12]

Is He Angry Enough?

Do you get the impression that Mr. Warner is angry, due to his own dogmatism? If not, read his comments again. His attitude and demeanor do nothing, except to spawn arrogance within him. Warner would likely assert that he is defending the gospel, and as such, has every right to refer to "heretics" the way he does. However, this presupposes, of course, that he is correct in his own particular beliefs. Certainly, he would not hesitate to state unequivocally, that he is right.

It is difficult to read comments like Warner's because they are so off-putting. There is little (if anything), which promotes a spirit of unity in love. Warner has become the teacher, and as such, has little patience with people who do not believe as he believes, accepting his teaching as the truth.

Individuals like Tim Warner seem to view PreTrib Rapturists as if they were members of cults. Even so, let us consider how their approach to a member of a true cult might work. Would we really expect a Mormon, a Jehovah's Witness, or some other individual involved in a cult, to be willing to listen to us, if we went off on a tirade every time we came to a point of disagreement? Certainly not. Solomon's words speak to this in numerous places. One such place is found in Proverbs 25:15, "*Through patience a ruler can be persuaded,*

---

[12] Email from Tim Warner dated 07/11/2009 received at 10:52pm

and a soft tongue can break a bone." Paul states that we are to present the gospel in love and with a humble spirit.

> *"I, therefore, the prisoner for the Lord, urge you to live worthily of the calling with which you have been called, with all humility and gentleness, with patience, bearing with one another in love, making every effort to keep the unity of the Spirit in the bond of peace. There is one body and one Spirit, just as you too were called to the one hope of your calling, one Lord, one faith, one baptism, one God and Father of all, who is over all and through all and in all,"* (Ephesians 4:1-6, NET Bible)

Naturally, we witness those times in the epistles where Paul came off a bit acerbically, toward those who seemed to him, to not only be repudiating the gospel, but attempting to keep others from hearing it as well. We can understand his frustration, and resultant demeanor, which stemmed from it.

However, I, for one, feel much more comfortable allowing Jesus to overturn the tables of the moneychangers, and Paul to become angered enough to say, *"I wish those agitators would go so far as to castrate themselves!"* (Galatians 5:12 NET) I do not believe that this gives us, as God's children (and *non*-apostles!), the right to condemn others, or treat them in a demeaning way.

Nevertheless, Warner's quotes from a few pages prior are presented as fact, though, in reality, they are *suspect*. First of all, his comment that *"Almost all of the Reformation era believers held to 'historicism,' the belief that the 'tribulation' covers 1260 years (from the rise of the Roman Catholic Church to the second coming)..."* turns out to mean absolutely *nothing*. He is attempting to prove that immanency played no part in the beliefs of the Reformers. Again though, what does that have to do with anything?

It is a well-known fact of history, that the Roman Catholic Church's doctrines in many areas were not only repugnant, but also biblically inaccurate. This is the reason for Luther's 95 Theses. The fact that the Roman Catholic Church adopted their views of Eschatology from Augustine's *allegorical* views only proves that the Roman Catholic Church was successful for hundreds of years in suppressing and censoring views with which they did not agree.

Besides, if one considers the entirety of church history, from the very start of the church, a number of interesting things can be easily observed (the following information is taken from Dwight D. Pentecost's *Things to Come*, in which he quotes from *The Progress of Dogma*, by James Orr):

- *"The history of dogma, as you speedily discover is simply the system of theology spread out through the centuries…*
- *"The second century in the history of the Church – what was that? The age of Apologetics and of the vindication of the five fundamental ideas of all religion – of the Christian especially – in conflict with Paganism and with the Gnostics.*
- *"We pass to the next stage in the development, and what do we find there? Just what comes next in the theological system – Theology Proper – the Christian doctrine of God, and specially the doctrine of the Trinity. This period is covered by Monarchian, Arian, and Macedonian controversies of the third and fourth centuries.*
- *"What comes next? As in the logical system theology is succeeded by Anthropology, so in the history of dogma the controversies I have named are followed in the beginning of the fifth century by Augustinian and Pelagian controversies, in which…the centre of interest shifts from God to man.*
- *"From the time of Augustine's death we see the Church entering on that long and distracting series of controversies known as Christological – Nestorian, Eutychian, Monophysite, Monothe-*

*lite – which kept it in continual ferment, and rent it with the
most unchristlike passions during the fifth and sixth, on even till
near the end of the seventh, centuries...*

- *"What now shall I say of the remaining branch of the theological
system, the Eschatological? An Eschatology, indeed, there
was in the early Church, but it was not theologically conceived;
and a Mythical Eschatology there was in the Mediaeval Church
– an Eschatology of Heaven, Hell, and Purgatory...but the Reformation
swept this away, and, with its sharply contrasted
states of bliss and woe, can hardly be said to have pout anything
in its place, or even to have faced very distinctly the difficulties
of the problem..."*[13]

Pentecost comments on the above, by stating, *"This whole concept of
the progress of dogma would be our strongest argument against the
posttribulation rapturist who argues that the doctrine must be rejected
because it was not clearly taught in the early church."*[14]

Based on this, the fact that we have even *one* document from the first,
second, or third centuries that clearly states a PreTrib Rapture, is
remarkable, in and of itself! The Pseudo-Ephraem document is the
single greatest proof that at least *someone* outside of the Bible in the
early days of the Church, believed in a rapture of the Church *prior* to
the Tribulation. Yet, as one person states, *"I think it is amazing evidence
against Jeffrey's position that in over ten years of research this is
all that he could find. This shows that, even if Pseudo-Ephraem was a
pre-tribulationist, this was the exception, not the rule."*[15]

So on one hand, Posttribulationalists, and others castigate and condemn
the PreTrib Rapturist for a *lack of evidence* from the early
Church. Yet, when evidence is located, it is downplayed, as if it does

---

[13] Dwight D. Pentecost *Things to Come* (Grand Rapids Academie Books 1958), 167
[14] Ibid, 168
[15] http://www.apostolic.net/biblicalstudies/post/link7.htm

not exist. Others write articles and/or books on the subject, in an attempt to convince everyone that there is no validity in the Pseudo-Ephraem document altogether.

Even during Paul's day, the controversies surrounding Jesus had to do with either His lack of full deity, or His lack of full humanity, or some other aspect related to Him and/or salvation. Paul clearly spent time dealing with this in such epistles as Galatians and Ephesians. John also dealt with these subjects in his gospel account, as well as his epistles. James and Peter also deal with aspects of these controversies.

It should not be hard to understand that Eschatology was simply not a major concern. Certainly, as history proves, it took centuries for the Church to establish the doctrine of Eschatology. Aside from a belief in an imminent return, Eschatology in and of itself was simply not a high priority.

Does Imminency Mean "Any Moment"?
It should seem clear that believers of the first, second and even the third century had a view of an *imminent* return of Christ. We gain this from the Scripture itself:

- John 14:2-3
- 1 Corinthians 1:7
- Philippians 3:20-21
- 1 Thessalonians 1:9-10; 4:16-17; 5:5-9
- Titus 2:13
- James 5:8-9
- Revelation 3:10; 22:17-22

Problems, Concerns, and Complaints About Imminency?
Another individual, C. H. Fisher, in his ebook called *The Pretribulational Rapture*, chapter twelve, spends a good deal of time accusing the PreTrib Rapturist of finding imminency in the gospel of Matthew

and Mark. Fisher asks whether Jesus Himself taught imminency. Referring to this, he then dogmatically states, *"If He did, we should be able to find abundant scriptures that declare this teaching clearly. In fact, there are none. That's right, there is not one scripture to support the doctrine of imminency for the entirety of the Church's existence on earth. Imminency is the idea that the Parousia of Christ Jesus could occur at any moment."*[16]

If you are confused after reading his comments above, you are not the only one. Fisher is confused about a number of things related to the Rapture and the Second Coming and unfortunately, mixes them as if they are the same. He does this because he is a Posttribulationalist; one who believes that the Rapture occurs at the same time the Lord returns. He then spends a good deal of time highlighting passages from the Olivet Discourse in both Matthew and Mark. The problem though is for the PreTrib Rapturist, these passages highlight Christ's actual *Second Coming*, not the Rapture. Moreover, even though Fisher understands that the PreTrib Rapturist makes a distinction between Israel and the Church, he seems to be unaware that for the PreTrib Rapturist, Christ's Olivet Discourse essentially speaks to the nation of Israel, almost entirely, not the Church.

It is from these passages that the Posttribulationalist attempts to show that the Church will go through the Tribulation. However, since the passage is addressed to the nation of Israel, and not the Church, it would only be logical to understand that Christ is speaking of the fact that it is the *nation of Israel* that will experience the Tribulation period, and not the Church. Since Posttribulationalists make *no* distinction between the Church and Israel, passages such as those found in John 15 and 16 are used to support their contention that the Church will go through the Tribulation. However, unless the passage is allegorized, it cannot refer to the Church at all.

---

[16] http://truthkeepers.com/chapter_twelve.htm

Pentecost explains, "*Scripture abounds in promises that Israel will be brought into a time of purging to prepare them as a nation for the millennium to follow the advent of Messiah. However, since Israel is to be distinguished from the church in the economy of God, those scriptures which promise tribulation to Israel can not be made to teach that the church is to experience the tribulation period. Israel and the church are two distinct entities in the plan of God and must so be regarded.*"[17]

Someone may ask *why* the Church and Israel are kept separate. Does this not mean that there is a unique plan of salvation for each? No, it would not mean that, because we know that Scripture teaches that from Adam and Eve to the very last individual ever born in human history future, salvation is the same for all, without distinction, or respecter of persons; it is by grace, through faith, in Christ. It has never been different, in spite of what Covenant Theologians and others might say about a Covenant of Works, and a Covenant of Grace.

Fisher errs in his understanding of where the PreTrib Rapturist gains understanding of the doctrine of Imminency, in the first place. It is without a doubt, *not* in Matthew 24 or Mark 13. Further trouble originates in the way in which the Posttribulationalist interprets areas of Daniel 9. Often these are allegorized to mean longer periods than Daniel intended. Because of the way these 70 weeks of Daniel 9 are interpreted by Posttribulationalists, *Christ* is often seen as the one who enters into a covenant with Israel at the beginning of the 70th week. The covenant is then broken in the "middle" of the week, by Christ's crucifixion. Yet, why are certain "weeks" of the 70 weeks interpreted, or understood in literal terms of 7 years, while other "weeks" are interpreted as being much longer periods? It does not make logical sense how the same word in the same section of Scripture can refer to one length of time, and then another length of time.

---

[17] Dwight D. Pentecost *Things to Come* (Grand Rapids Academie Books 1958), 170

Allegorizing What Should Not Be Allegorized

Regarding those passages then which refer to Israel's national salvation, *following* the 70th week, Posttribulationalists point to the Church. For them, the Church is the fulfillment of passages like Daniel and elsewhere, related to Israel's salvation. One can easily see how these passages of Scripture take on a new meaning through the indiscriminate use of allegory.

However, more importantly, the lack of understanding regarding the pronoun "he" in Daniel 9:27, and who it actually refers to there is telling. *"Again, the "he" of Daniel 9:27 must have as its antecedent 'the prince that shall come' of the preceding verse. Because this one is related to the people who destroyed the city and the sanctuary, that is the Romans, this one confirming the covenant can not be Christ, but must be the man of sin, spoken of by Christ (Matt. 24:15), by Paul (2 Thess. 2), and John (Rev. 13), who will make a false covenant with Israel. The fact that sacrifices and oblation* **continued** *after the death of Christ until the year 70 A.D. would point out the fact that it was not Christ who caused these sacrifices to terminate. It is interesting to note that the Lord, in that great eschatological passage dealing with the future of Israel (Matt. 24-25),* **speaks of a yet future fulfillment of Daniel's prophecy (Matt. 24:15) after His death.**"[18] (emphasis added)

What is also clear is that for the Posttribulationalist, there seems to be absolutely *no* distinction made between an understanding of Christ coming *soon,* and Christ's coming as *imminent.* It should be plainly obvious that Scripture does not teach that the Lord's coming is soon. It teaches that His coming should be expected to occur at any time. There is a huge difference between these notions, yet Fisher himself apparently does not see or understand the distinction, for he obviously believes that when the PreTrib Rapturist speaks of the Lord's coming as imminent, he takes that to mean that the idea of His *soon* coming is being espoused. This is not the case.

---

[18] Dwight D. Pentecost *Things to Come* (Grand Rapids Academie Books 1958), 172

Does Imminent Mean Soon?

Let me try to illustrate. I am in college class, and the professor states something like, *"Folks, we have a guest speaker today, as I mentioned the last time we were together. He will be speaking on the subject of anarchy in the 21ˢᵗ century, and as soon as he arrives, we will turn the floor over to him. Until then, let's open our books to page 578 and continue our discussion from last Thursday."*

Therefore, on one hand, we are expecting this guest speaker to appear *at any moment*, and in this case, it is also *soon*. However, let us say that we see the guest speaker arrive just outside the class window. He stops outside the door, and begins a conversation with another individual. We have no idea how long this conversation will go on, so even though we might be *tempted* to think in terms of his soon arrival into our class, it may *not* be that soon.

One thing *is* clear though, and that is that his arrival to the inside of the room is *imminent*, because it could happen at any moment. The guest speaker is in a position – right outside the door – which allows him to enter our classroom *at any moment*, and because of this, it places his arrival to our class as *imminent*.

Fisher comments on imminency by stating, *"In the following scripture we are told that we should follow a certain procedure in order to be aware of His coming. It is not the fig tree we are told to watch, but to employ the method of determining the signs that indicate what is about to occur. As we see the signs of leaves in the fig tree, we know that summer is approaching. Jesus used other metaphors in much the same way."*[19]

However, what Fisher does not realize is that he has just *proven* the doctrine of imminency. If it is true what Fisher above states (and I would for one, agree with most of what he states), then what could

---

[19] http://truthkeepers.com/chapter_twelve.htm

every other individual who refers to the fact that we await our Savior, that He stands at the gate, or door, and that His coming is *imminent* actually mean, if not that Christ could return at any moment? In other words, many of the passages that speak of His return, have absolutely no date or time associated with them (cf. 1 Peter 3:3-4; James 5:8; 1 Timothy 6:14). They do not speak of His return as being *soon*, as much as they speak of it as being *imminent.*

James 5:8 in the NET version states, "*You also be patient and strengthen your hearts, for the Lord's return is near.*"

Titus 2:13 from the NET states, "*as we wait for the happy fulfillment of our hope in the glorious appearing of our great God and Savior, Jesus Christ.*"

1 Thessalonians 5:6, also from the NET, states, "*So then we must not sleep as the rest, but must stay alert and sober.*"

It should make absolute sense that if the Church was *Premillennial* in position, then their view of the fact that Lord could come at any moment, meant, it *could occur at any time*, but not necessarily that His coming was *soon*.

There would have been absolutely no point in constantly reminding everyone that the day or hour of the Lord's return is unknown, implying that it could occur *at any moment*, if in point of fact, it could *not* occur at any moment!

Chapter 2
Those Early Church Fathers

Take the time to read just about any of the early church fathers. There, you will find a mix of commentary, with Scripture, or even a somewhat rambling mix of generalized, rewritten Scripture, with their commentary.

Often, their own understanding seemed to be lacking with respect to what was going to occur, and I believe the reason for that is because they did not *know*. In fact, a number of them appeared *not* to be Rapturists at all. They seemed to expect to face the Antichrist, as if they were going to march out onto the field of battle, with weapons, and stand against him in the power of the Lord. When the smoked clears, Christ will have returned, and the Antichrist will be dead. The ironic part is that the plain scenario in Revelation shows that no Christian stands against Antichrist and his armies. They are all running and hiding from him! Christ returns *with* His saints, and He vanquishes this enemy.

The Second Coming Is the Rapture?

The Posttribulationalist believes generally that *as* Jesus returns, the rapture occurs. At that point, all believers are translated to meet Christ, and return with Him to earth, as He alone defeats the Antichrist. This makes little sense and one cannot help but wonder why, at that point, in time, there even *needs* to be a rapture, if the point is to simply immediately return to earth where you were one millionth of a second previously?

That aside, it is also clear that there was a belief in an imminency; that Christ's return could occur at any moment. This is obvious from simply perusing Paul's epistles, though Posttribulationalists and others attempt to negate his meaning.

There is a great deal of Old Testament imagery in the writings of the early church fathers. As the physical and real battles unfolded on the plains, or even in the mountains at times, so too, did these early church fathers expect to stand in formation with other believers, against the coming Antichrist.

As mentioned previously, it took hundreds of years for doctrines such as the Trinity, the deity of Christ and salvation apart from works, to become more fully ensconced as official Church doctrine. It appears obvious though, that Eschatology was not high on the list of priorities. To these godly men, their marching orders consisted of living a godly life, as the end approached.

As time went on, it becomes clear though, that there were points in history when specific doctrines came to the fore, and were dealt with at that time. It is probable that one of the reasons Eschatology was not dealt with for centuries, has more to do with the fact that having a *wrong* view of how everything would work itself out as the End approached, really had no bearing on one's salvation, (nor does it still).

So, why do people consider a wrong view today regarding Eschatology to be heretical, to the point that it is thought to impinge upon the salvation of an individual? In my opinion, I believe people often think in these terms today, because they often *overstate*, or *overemphasize* the overall importance Eschatology. Do not get me wrong; Eschatology *is* important; because it *should* affect the way we live today. However, it is certainly not as important as salvation.

The other reason people tend to view the PreTrib Rapture position (as well as Dispensationalism, in some cases), as heretical, is because at least some of these folks disagree about eternal security of believers. As stated, I believe that eternal security is exactly that: eternal and secure. There is nothing we can do to lose our salvation. Nothing. Let me add, that for the authentic Christian, though they will fall at times, their overall direction is to move continually closer to Christ. This is something that is brought about by the indwelling presence of the Holy Spirit. He elects, He saves, and He conforms us to His image. Our job is to *cooperate* in the process, my submitting to His will.

It makes sense then, that for those folks who erroneously *do* believe that salvation can be lost, doctrines such as *imminency*, or *PreTrib Rapture*, are thought to cause Christians to become confused enough, so that they will become lazy, and immature in the faith. The result – they believe - is a complete lack of preparation for the coming End Times holocaust. They are ruling out God's sovereignty though, which to them, seems to play no role in the salvation of the Christian.

Is the PreTrib Rapture Merely an Escape Clause?

As I have also stated, those Christians who view the PreTrib Rapture as some type of escape clause, likely already exhibited this attitude and demeanor in their lives *prior* to adopting the PreTrib Rapture position. It cannot be logically assumed that a belief in a PreTrib Rapture *caused* this development in their lives.

Consider the fact that the average American Christian today is one consumed by materialism. The latest and greatest car or home is needed. Continuing to move up the company ladder is important to them. Having the best clothing, or being able to take trips to the Bahamas, or hobnobbing with the rich and famous, etc., are all things to which they seek.

Along those same lines, when this same average Christian is asked their view of the End Times, or specifically, of the Rapture, they will likely respond with something like, *"What's the Rapture?" The End Times; what's that?"*

Though the Bible is the highest selling book, it is the least read. Everyone has one, but the cover is rarely opened. The average Christian cannot state that there are 66 books in the entire Bible, or that 27 of them compose the New Testament, while 39 make up the Old. They cannot even name them in order.

The average churchgoer has memorized very few Bible verses, if any. They have no clue what the Bible is about, except in very general terms (God vs. Satan; God wins. End of story.). Their desire to read and study the Bible is severely lacking.

If these church-going, professing Christians were asked to name the main highlights of the book of Genesis, for instance, they would perhaps relate something like *"God created everything, then there was Adam and Eve. They were in the Garden of Eden, and they sinned.*

There was a flood and a guy named Noah. I think Abraham was in it too."

Ask these same individuals to explain the books of 1 and 2 Samuel, or the book of Joel, or Isaiah, or Ezekiel, and their face would adopt a blank look. They cannot do it, because they have not studied it.

Go a step further, and question the same church-going individuals about J. N. Darby, or C. I. Scofield, and the likely reply would be on the something along the lines of a blank expression. They have *no* clue. None. Yet, to hear some like Dave MacPherson tell it, these two men were the catalyst in subverting the generally accepted, normative Posttribulational doctrine of the entire church up until that time!

Entertainment is Key for the Modern Christian
The average church attendee is more interested in having a social hour at church (if and when they attend). They want the music to be upbeat. They want the sermons to be upbeat...and *short!* They do not want to hear about *sin*, or Christ's atonement, unless it can be done without making them feel as though they need to do something like submit to Him. These accidental church attendees, wants to *feel* good about themselves and their lives. They do not want to be made to feel as though life can, or will get tough. They do not want to hear anything about the End Times, because that is too scary.

In short, today's church-going individual wants to be comfortable. They want to hear and know that they are fine, now. God loves them as they are, and does not expect them to change. It will all work out in the end, and it is going to go from good to better, to best! However, this is *not* what the early church fathers taught or believed, nor is it what the Bible teaches. To the early members of the Church, the coming of Christ was *imminent*; meaning, it could occur any day, in spite of what Posttribulationalists believe. The signs that they may point to, which they believe signals Christ's return are exactly that - signaling His Second Coming. However, there are *no* signs at all for the Rapture of the saints, and this is clear in Paul's letter to the Thessalonian believers.

Clement had some interesting things to say, as did many of the Early Church Fathers. From the following statements, we gain a sense of how Clement viewed the coming of the Lord:

"2Clem 11:7
If therefore we shalt have wrought righteousness in the sight of God, we shalt enter into His kingdom and shall receive the promises which ear hath not heard nor eye seen, nor eye seen, neither hath it entered into the heart of man.

2Clem 12:1
Let us therefore await the kingdom of God betimes in love and righteousness, since we know not the day of God's appearing.

2Clem 12:2
For the Lord Himself, being asked by a certain person when his kingdom would come, said, When the two shall be one, and the outside as the inside, and the male with the female, neither male or female.

2Clem 12:3
Now the two are one, when we speak truth among ourselves, and in two bodies there shall be one soul without dissimulation.

2Clem 12:4
And by the outside as the inside He meaneth this: by the inside he meaneth the soul and by the outside the body. Therefore in like manner as thy body appeareth, so also let thy soul be manifest by its good works."[20]

What is interesting regarding the above is that in 2 Clement 12:1, he states that we should be busy waiting for the Kingdom of God, at all

---

[20] http://www.earlychristianwritings.com/text/2clement-lightfoot.html

times, because we do not know the day of God's appearing. He explains that statement by saying (in a reference to Galatians 3:26-28), since the *two have become one*, then God's kingdom could literally arrive at any day; any time. This does *not* prove a PreTrib Rapture, and that is not what we are discussing. We are discussing the early Church's understanding of *imminence.*

The Didache, as well as other early writings of the Church, display a *sense of imminency*, in that they expected the return of Christ at any time. In fact, when reading many of the documents produced by the early church fathers, it becomes apparent that for most of them, the idea that the Lord could return at any moment, is an integral part of what they believed and taught.

The Term "Saint"

In all likelihood, what probably confuses people is the use of the term "saints" as used of believers, during the Tribulation/Great Tribulation. Though the Church, in my view, has been Raptured before this seven-year time span, it is unambiguous from Scripture that many will be saved during that time of trouble. It should actually surprise no one, yet because this fact exists, people then believe that the Rapture could *not* have occurred beforehand, and if it did, then how did these "saints" get in the Tribulation? It appears to be something beyond their ability to comprehend. Yet, the reality is simple. The Rapture occurred, the Church (Bride of Christ) was taken, and many of those who were not taken, while not Christians, actually attended and were involved in the visible Church! Therefore, they had heard the preaching and teaching on the End Times and the Rapture. Now that it had occurred, and they did not go, they finally realized (to their chagrin and fear), that they were not authentic Christians. Now, however, they will not make that mistake again! Because there are saints in the Tribulation period, does not contradict or negate the teaching of the Bible on the PreTrib Rapture. It also does not negate or preclude the concept of imminency.

When you consider the fact that the oft repeated phrase "the Lord could come at any moment," or some derivative of it, was meant to be understood in terms of His *nearness*, and if He was *near*, then He could arrive at any moment. The verses below express this thought (all quoted from the NET; emphasis added):

"Let everyone see your gentleness. ***The Lord is near!****"* (Philippians 4:5)

"Do not grumble against one another, brothers and sisters, so that you may not be judged. ***See, the judge stands before the gates!****"* (James 5:9)

"For the culmination of all things is near. *So be self-controlled and sober-minded for the sake of prayer."* (1 Peter 4:7)

"I am coming soon. *Hold on to what you have so that no one can take away your crown."* (Revelation 3:11)

Many verses communicate imminence in the Bible. This is not a fabricated concept, or doctrine, as C. H. Fisher and others would have us believe. 1 John 3:2-3, along with many other verses, bear this out (from the NET):

"Dear friends, we are God's children now, and what we will be has not yet been revealed. We know that whenever it is revealed we will be like him, because we will see him just as he is. And everyone who has this hope focused on him purifies himself, just as Jesus is pure)."

John is encouraging all who are in Christ (authentic Christians), to consider what Christ is like *now*, in His glorified Body, in the eternal state. We should think of Him, because when we *see* Him, we will have instantly become like Him. John tells us that this type of thinking purifies the individual. How? By clearing our minds of the things that can easily entangle us with the problems of this world, it is easier to focus on our hope in Christ Jesus!

Therefore, when done correctly, understanding what imminence actually means, places us in the mental position of considering the heavenly things. Does not Paul say the same thing?

"Therefore, if you have been raised with Christ, keep seeking the things above, where Christ is, seated at the right hand of God. Keep thinking about things above, not things on the earth, for you have died and your life is hidden with Christ in God. When Christ (who is your life) appears, then you too will be revealed in glory with him."

The above passage from Colossians 3:1-4, expresses the concept of *dwelling on* or *thinking about* those things which are *above*, because by doing so, rather than make us feel like we can live any way we want to live (antinomianism) here and now, we will instead, be encouraged to *"put to death whatever in your nature belongs to the earth: sexual immorality, impurity, shameful passion, evil desire, and greed which is idolatry,"* (v. 5). This is the *actual* result of dwelling on our being in Christ's physical presence!

Weak-Kneed and Immature

It is often stated that those who believe in a PreTrib Rapture position, become weak-kneed, immature Christians, who live as they want to live, doing whatever they want to do, pleasing self, displeasing God. Statements like this make no sense. If a person is correctly viewing the future dwelling with Christ, how could that *possibly* be the impetus for living the lazy, carnal life that is exhibited in Paul's first letter to the Corinthian believers? It honestly cannot.

Those "Christians," who are now living a carnal life, with absolutely no concern for their sin (and not understanding how despicable it is to God), have no real understanding of what it means to be an *authentic* Christian. If they are living that way, the PreTrib Rapture position did not created that. It is their lack of commitment to the Lord, from beginning to end that created that. There has likely been no spiritual transaction. Their life has not been exchanged for the eternal life of Christ. If it has, then they have yet to comprehend the reality of the cross and the implications of living a carnal life.

Paul takes such pains to explain this in Galatians and the Corinthian believers. While the fact that salvation is absolutely free, and that no one can do anything to earn any part of it, it does *not* mean that we are allowed to live a life any way we wish to live, simply because we are somehow "once saved, always saved." I personally believe in eternal security, and I do so because I believe it is taught clearly in God's Word. The fact that people take advantage by misunderstanding the ramifications of eternal security is *not* the fault of the doctrine itself, but the fault of those who misunderstand it. Their abuse of the doctrine does not negate it.

Getting back to the doctrine of *imminency*, it would be helpful to discover what the English word actually means. Does it connect with the idea that the Rapture could happen at any moment, or does it negate the biblical understanding?

"ready to take place; hanging threateningly over one's head," from the Merriam-Webster dictionary[21]

"likely to occur at any moment; impending: (Her death is imminent)," from Dictionary.com[22]

"close in time; about to occur," from Dictionary of Definitions[23]

The difficulty with this word, as with so many in the English (or any), language, is that because *imminent* is similar in nature to *soon*, the words are sometimes taken to mean the same thing, but this is certainly not the case.

Consider these two sentences:

---

[21] http://www.merriam-webster.com/dictionary/imminent
[22] http://dictionary.reference.com/browse/imminent
[23] http://www.dictionaryofdefinitions.com/what-is-the-definition-of-imminent.html

*The dark clouds were signaling an **imminent** rain storm.*
*The weather forecast said to expect rain **soon**.*

For the sake of argument, let us say that a weather forecaster never makes a mistake. Every time they forecast the weather, they are right on. In that case, while our first sentence speaks of the *possibility* of rain occurring at any moment, the second sentence speaks of the fact that rain will begin *soon*, or *in the near future*.

Synonyms for the word *imminent* make this point even more clear:

"about to happen, approaching, brewing, close, coming, expectant, fast-approaching, following, forthcoming, gathering, handwriting-on-the-wall, immediate, impending, in store, in the air, in the cards, in the offing, in the wind, in view, ineluctable, inescapable, inevasible, inevitable, likely, looming, menacing, near, nearing, next, nigh, on its way, on the horizon, on the verge, overhanging, possible, probable, see it coming, threatening, to come, unavoidable, inescapable"[24]

Soon, or Imminent?

With the exception of the first phrase – *about to happen* – none of the related synonyms have *soon* in view. They speak of something that is *near* and could happen at any time. The other thing about imminent is that even though something is imminent, it does not have to occur, at least at that point in time. Not so with the word *soon*. When the word *soon* is used in a sentence, it points to the fact that the event referenced *will happen shortly*.

Tim Warner makes a sweeping generalization by stating that (still referring to Grant Jeffrey's book on the Apocalypse), *"A perfect example of these blatant lies are the claims that when someone used the word "rapture" that must make them a pretribulationist. Hogwash! I*

---

[24] http://thesaurus.reference.com/browse/imminent

use the word "rapture" too, and I am no pretribulationist. I would wager that most in that list are the same kind of revisionism." [25]

The trouble with the above comment, as with much of the material that Warner presents, is that it is virtually *devoid* of verifiable documentation. Beyond this, his argument completely ignores *context*. However, who said that those who have used the word "rapture" in the past must be because they are Pretribulationalists? It would be good to know that it is verifiable. Maybe it is, but without the documentation, it is difficult, if not impossible to know exactly whom Warner is referring to with that comment. He also appears to be *assuming* that "most in the list are of the same kind of revisionism," yet he obviously has not bothered to check, nor has he provided documentation for the claim.

Just because Warner himself uses the word "rapture" (with a meaning *other* than indicating a PreTrib Rapture), this fact has absolutely no bearing on the first century's use of the word, as pertaining to the Church. There is no connection whatsoever. The actual crux of the matter is in the *meaning* of the word *imminent* or similar words used in Scripture. Meanings cannot be determined in a vacuum. Word studies are valuable, as far as they go, but they do not provide the *entirety* of meaning. The meaning *must* be considered within its *context.*

Examples of Context
If I am in a taxi, and I say to the driver, *"Please turn left at the next intersection,"* I would expect him to turn left at the next intersection. Upon arriving at my destination, I look through my wallet to find that I am short of cash, which may lead me to say, *"I only have fifteen dollars left..."* which then might force me to reach for, and offer my ATM Debit card as payment.

---

[25] Email from Tim Warner dated 07/11/2009 received at 10:52pm; on file

In the above examples, the word *left* was used in both. However, it should be clear that the word does *not* mean the same thing in both examples. What determines the meaning in each case? It is the *context*.

In another example, we have the word *apostle*. At its root, it means, "sent one." This is exactly what they were; sent ones. Christ picked them, trained them, and then sent them. The trouble is when I hear people saying that "so and so is an apostle," or even when people *themselves* seem to have designated themselves as apostles. On one hand, all Christians can state that we are in some sense, apostles, because we are sent because of the Great Commission.

However, can anyone today, really be appointed (by self, or otherwise), an actual apostle, as in Paul, Matthew, James, John, Andrew, etc.? No, I don't believe so and the verification of that is found in Revelation when it is pointed out to John that the *12 gates* have the names of the *12 apostles* on them (cf. Revelation 21). Those original apostles (even including Paul), were *handpicked* by Jesus Christ. He picked them, they learned from Him, as disciples, and then He personally commissioned them. In spite of what some may believe, we *cannot* be actual apostles today. So, in spite of the fact that the essential meaning of the word *apostle* means *sent one,* it also can mean much more than that, depending upon context.

It is the same with the word *church*. Though some argue that the word used in the Old Testament is the word *ekklesia*, and it is the same (in the Greek), for the Church in the New Testament, this does *not* prove a connection. It is just as likely that the word *ekklesia*, which meant a *congregation*, was simply adopted to describe the Church of the New Testament. Certainly, there is no way at all that the *mystery, which* Paul explained (making one man out of the two), could be in any way, shape or form, said to relate to Israel, as the *ekklesia* in the Old Testament.

Word studies are fine, as far as they go, but the meat of a word, or a phrase's meaning, is found in the *context*. How is the word being used *at the time*? It does not matter what the word means five sentences before it, unless the *exact same context* exists (remember *left*, and *left* – same word, two different applications, based solely on context).

With respect to imminency, many things have been said about it; some good, some bad, but all have an opinion. C. H. Fisher contends that, *"One of [the] spin-off doctrines that pretribulation rapturists have invented is the doctrine of Imminency. They use the argument that any doctrine that has the church going through the tribulation period takes away the imminency of Jesus' coming."*[26]

"PreTrib Rapture is Wrong, Therefore Imminency is Wrong"
Fisher continues, by analyzing Dave Hunt's comments related to imminency, stating, *"A major problem with this argument is that the doctrine of Imminency is not valid Bible doctrine and would not exist if it were not for PTR. If we get rid of PTR, that solves the problem of imminency. In other words, get rid of the dog that brought the fleas...It is also an example of one error leading to another. Pretribulation Rapturism hangs its flag on the doctrine of imminency. This means they have to interpret the scriptures in a way that fortifies Pretribulation Rapture."*[27]

It is quickly apparent that not only does Fisher believe that the doctrine of imminency (in this case, as defined by the Posttrib Rapturist), is *not* Scriptural, but to him, it belongs in the category of manufactured doctrine. He has made sweeping generalizations, which ultimately have no bearing in truth.

There *is* a doctrine of Imminence, and it *is* a biblical doctrine. As we have seen, there is plenty of evidence for it (some of which we have

---

[26] http://truthkeepers.com/chapter_twelve.htm
[27] http://truthkeepers.com/chapter_twelve.htm

already presented), to be found in Scripture, if folks are simply willing to see Scripture as it presents itself. Saying that the doctrine does not exist is patently false...unless the person has replaced the word *imminence* with *soon*. In that case, the person would be applying the wrong meaning to the word imminent.

There is a great deal of accusation and condemnation regarding the PreTrib Rapture position. It has been called something that came from the pit of hell, heresy, deception, and much more. Why? All because people wrongly believe that, the doctrine of the PreTrib Rapture provides a "free pass" to avoid impending Wrath of God. Nothing could be further from the truth, especially if one considers the fact that even in 2009, Christians are still literally martyred (yes, *KILLED*), for their faith often. We have already presented data on this.

What is the End Goal of Being an Authentic Christian?
Authentic Christians today are not shrinking from death or torture because they may believe that a Rapture will occur prior to the Tribulation. Maybe Christians in America might shrink from it, but that is *still* not the fault of the PreTrib Rapture, and has everything to do with how a Christian lives their life on a daily basis, amidst the swill of raunchy TV, movies, music and more. *That* is what is making people become lazy, overindulgent, superficial "Christians." That, coupled with the Emergent Church, which plays right into their hands, has given professing Christians reason to become the exact opposite of what the Fruit of the Spirit entails.

Still not convinced? Okay, then go back and read Luke 12:13-21. It deals with the rich landowner. There are many lessons in this parable, but it would suffice to point out only one. Luke 12:20 states (from the NET), "But God said to him, '*You fool! This very night your life will be demanded back from you, but who will get what you have prepared for yourself?*'" The point is simple. We are to live *every* day as if it is our last on this earth.

We can argue all we want about a *Pre-Trib*, a *Posttrib*, a *Pre-Wrath*, a *Mid-Trib*, a *No-Trib*, or a *Who Cares-Trib Rapture*, but the reality is that even if there *is* a PreTrib Rapture, how many people living today will be alive to experience it? It may not occur for decades or centuries. We do *not* know when the last day that God has appointed for us, will arrive. In that sense, the end of our life is also <u>always</u> *imminent*. While it would not be correct for me to say that the end of my life is soon (since I do not know), I am correct in stating that it is *imminent*, as I am always only one breath away from it. I may be driving my car this afternoon, and become involved in an accident in which I will be killed. My death is still *imminent*, even if that does not occur.

Last November 2, 2008, I received a phone call from my sister's son-in-law. It was certainly an unexpected one, as he rarely called. I immediately knew something was up. He explained that my sister had collapsed in the garage, and it did not look good, so the hospital indicated it would be a good time to call family. I knew my sister had been tired, and there were a few health problems, but I never envisioned a total collapse with a possible death!

I flew back there and stayed with her and her husband and son. She never regained consciousness, and simply slipped away to the Lord one early morning about 1:30am. Just two days prior to that, I had talked with her and we had laughed as we normally did when we spoke with one another. It was always an uplifting conversation. The very day she died, I had sent her a text message, to which she never responded. My sister had no idea that she was going to have a massive heart attack and die. Certainly, I had no idea. However, she is gone, with the Lord, just like that.

Are you living as if it is *your* last day? You have *no* clue when your time is up, and the Lord will say, "Loved one, tonight your soul is required of you." You have *no* idea when that will happen. None! Your death is *always* imminent - *always*.

Chapter 3
Welcome to Your Last Day!

The issue we are discussing is *Eschatology*, or the *study of the Last Days*. A person's salvation – in spite of what some individuals believe – does *not* hinge upon a right view of the End Times. There are many godly men and women, who do not accept a PreTrib Rapture position, nor do they accept a Posttribulational position, yet their salvation is *sure*.

In Galatians, Paul was dealing with people who were attempting to *add* to the work of Christ. They believed it was fine to be a "Christian," however, the works of Judaism still applied and must be adhered to, as we have discussed earlier. Paul was rightly angered because he understood the gospel, and what Jesus had given up in order for salvation to be made available at all! Now, there were certain men who were attempting to twist the gospel message into something that it was not, by *adding works to it*. Paul could not allow this situation to continue. He knew how hard he had worked among the people in the province of Galatia to help them understand that salvation was a completely free gift.

Some today apparently believe that a wrong view of the End Times, results in an erosion of, and even a complete *loss* of salvation. On one hand, these individuals seem to want to protect and defend the gospel, yet on the other hand, they seem to be confused about just what it is they are actually attempting to protect, because they continually tie two separate areas of theology together.

The sad part of the entire problem, as shown for instance, by Warner's previous comments, is how often people like Thomas Ice, Grant Jeffrey and others are referred to as liars. For instance, Mr. Warner has produced a 15-page article in which he comments on the claims of Grant Jeffrey's book. Warner states that Jeffrey includes truncated versions of quotes, so that it merely *appears* as if these individuals are supporting a PreTrib Rapture position, when in fact, they do not (according to Warner).

We will certainly look at some of that as well, in our next chapter, but we must not neglect to note Mr. Warner's troubling attitude. We know from the statement of beliefs on his church's website[28] that Mr. Warner does not believe eternal security is a viable doctrine, taught in the Bible. Knowing this up front, it becomes clear *why* he interprets some of the writings by these authors of the early church, as he does. Beyond this, it is also apparent that to Warner, the use of the word "saints" means the same as the word "church." This is an as-

---

[28] http://www.oasischristianchurch.org/beliefs.html

sumption Warner arrives at, based on his predilection for Posttribulationalism.

Dave MacPherson's father, Dr. Norman Spurgeon MacPherson, warns against becoming prideful over a particular position and even makes the following statements in one of his own books; *"The subject matter of this book deals with the Christian's faith and hope. **But unless the spirit of love breathes on every page, the study will prove largely fruitless.***" [29] (emphasis added)

I would agree of course, as would most. Yet, why *does* a spirit of dissension exist within the Church over areas that are *peripheral* to the area of *salvation?* Interestingly enough, Dave MacPherson, Norman's son, falls prey to the same problem his father warns against, time after time, in any number of his books and articles he has written. However, all the while, he is busy pointing out this very flaw in someone else! Moreover, one of Norman MacPherson's own books makes a very dogmatic statement in its title; *Tell It Like It Will Be.*

It is sad that the father was not able to establish within his son a more temperate, loving spirit, than the one currently on display in his written works. To read the younger MacPherson, is to read works filled with sarcasm, and castigation. As James might likely state, *"Brothers, this should not be,"* (cf. James 3:10 NIV).

It's Not Taught in the Bible, Okay?! End of Story...
This declarative statement is used by most people when they come up against a position with which they do not agree. To make the statement *"It's not taught in the Bible,"* (or something similar), is a position of arrogance, even if it is true. It is designed to dissuade further discussion. It is what the atheist does when he states, "God does not exist!" Since there is no actual *proof* that can be pointed to, whereby any and every person would be dramatically convinced that God

---

[29] Norman Spurgeon MacPherson *Tell It Like It Will Be* (Albuquerque 1970 by author), 3

does exist, we are left to either walk away, praying for their salvation, or do our best to present the truth the Bible presents, or both.

Most of us have used this same statement, but apart from making us *sound* authoritative, it really serves no other purpose. In fact, it is off-putting and can often come across as arrogant; something Christians are to avoid. While we warn against being closed-minded, arrogant, unloving, and dogmatic, we all too often find ourselves guilty of these very things. Even when we *know* a doctrine to be true, the best course of action is stating the truth humbly.

The following statement by the elder MacPherson bears scrutiny, as it inadvertently applies to the situation for which this book is written, the PreTrib Rapture. Norman MacPherson states, "*If frequent reiteration of an unproved theory soon transforms it into an unshakable conviction, then we can understand the huge vogue that the theory of the double coming of Christ now enjoys in premillennial circles. It is commonly taught that Christ's coming is in two phases. First He comes secretly for His Church before the Tribulation, and a number of years later, perhaps seven, He comes publicly for purposes of judgment and the establishment of His Kingdom.*"[30]

The same could be said about his son's continual assertions that the PreTrib Rapture doctrine is false, or his assertions that Margaret MacDonald was the original vehicle through which the Rapture was made known. This very same thing could applied to the constant harangue that Dispensationalism receives for teaching two forms of salvation, which is does not. Constant repetition *seems* to yield truth.

The Second Advent involves *one* return of Jesus. The Rapture is not at all part of the Second Coming, since they are separated by at least

---

[30]

http://www.stpaulsbiblechurch.org/Triumph%20Through%20Tribulation.htm#III._ARG
UMENTS_OF_THE_PRE-TRIBULATION

seven years. As I say, we will delve more deeply into that in the appropriate time in this book.

When discussing the subject of the End Times, in biblical terms, it is becoming routine today to hear statements similar to the following: *"All the gloom and doom teachers and preachers are in it for the bucks!"* or *"The PreTrib Rapture position ignores and denies the reality of Christian suffering down through the ages by wanting to escape the coming persecution."*

Gloom and Doom for Profit

The above statements are often heard, with various degrees of rhetoric associated with them. They are made by those who generally disagree with "gloom and doom." They do not want to hear it. They ignore it in the Bible, passing it off as allegory, or something that has already happened in the past. They prefer to think of life in terms of it becoming better and better, until eventually, the time will be right for the Lord Jesus to step from heaven, and set up His kingdom on earth!

It is not unlike repeating the phrase "In every way, in every day, I'm getting better and better!" This is the where it appears that much of the visible Church is starting from; through involvement social work, which is believed to improve the state of the world. As such, it is believed that the world will become a better place and ultimately, the people who reside on planet earth will improve because their situations will have improved.

In the case of the Church, it is espoused that if the gloom and doom of the Bible is ignored and/or explained away, things will *be* brighter because they will *appear* brighter. Therefore, anyone found teaching or preaching a gloom or doom theology, is said to be one who holds back God's will from occurring. After all, if Jesus is depending upon humanity to actually cause things on earth to come to such a positive point in future history (allowing the Lord to return), then obviously, the "gloom and doomers" are simply acting as flies in the ointment. Never mind that the Bible certainly seems to offer a very gloomy picture of the future *prior* to His return.

Not too long ago, someone who disagreed with the PreTrib Rapture position accused me of profiting from my "false" doctrine. His exact words were, "*The fact is you profit by selling the false doctrine of PTR to the unwitting masses. Like the heretics in Ephesus that Paul exposed, you appear to be willing to do whatever it takes to preserve your means of income.*"[31] It is an interesting accusation, in and of itself. His real problem is the fact that I am "selling the false doctrine of PTR," which is the PreTrib Rapture position. Apparently, if you are Dave MacPherson, it is perfectly fine to publish books because MacPherson (according to the person with whom I have just quoted), publishes only the truth. Apparently, if you publish the 'truth,' it is fine to make a profit.

Stephen Quayle – Another Gloom and Doom Prophet

In another case, I was doing some research about Stephen Quayle, who has done quite a bit of research on Genesis 6, and specifically, the giants and Nephilim found therein. As usual, there is a great deal of disagreement over what Moses meant when he wrote those terms down in Genesis 6:4, and like anything else related to the Bible, there are those on both sides who use absolutes when describing and/or commenting on the situation. Their declarative statements are issued as a means of closing off dialogue and discussion. If someone says, "The Bible does NOT teach so and so, in any way, shape or form," then obviously those who disagree with that assumption are morons. Did they not just hear/read what was stated? "The Bible does NOT teach...!"

My point is that in researching the situation in Genesis 6, I came across a website that essentially castigates Quayle as someone who is

---

[31] Email received from C. H. Fisher, dated 07/12/2009 received at 7:41pm; on file

"profiting off of the error that he is preaching." So, here again, we have people who believe that because Quayle has attempted to offer insight into the entire Nephilim problem (through the publication of books), stating that we are seeing a renewal of it, "as it was in the days of Noah," and that things will only get worse, this constitutes doom and gloom. Since it is doom and gloom, those promoting it must be doing so in order to *profit* from that 'error.' Since they are profiting from it, they are swindle artists, not at all sincere about what they believe the Bible teaches.

For decades and decades, theologians have argued about PreTrib, Midtrib, Posttrib and other aspects of the Rapture and the End Times. However, because some have arrived at a conclusion they feel is fully justified and one they believe to be taught in Scripture, then anyone else who does not see it their way, is a heretic. Since they are heretics (and doom and gloom profiteers), then they can be treated as Jesus treated the Pharisees.

The only problem though is that many, if not most of us who believe in the PreTrib Rapture position, as well as the fact that Stephen Quayle may well have a point about the Nephilim, are *not* heretics at all. We believe in the substitutionary death of Christ by crucifixion and we believe that faith in that substitutionary death is the only way to *receive* salvation. Areas that are peripheral to salvation tend to be in the Eschatology area (study of End Times).

However, the arguments and protests from the "correct" crowd continue, against people who are PreTrib Rapturists. By espousing the PreTrib Rapture, we are seen as promoting a doctrine, which creates Christians who are completely unprepared to handle the coming cataclysm of the Tribulation/Great Tribulation. The so-called, natural result of believing and espousing the PreTrib Rapture as taught in the Bible, is to have thrown caution to the wind, living carnally. It is understood that before things get bad, the trump will sound, a voice will be heard, and Christians will be taken up in the clouds to be with Christ. THEN, the bad times will begin.

The people who actually believe that are probably not even authentic Christians to begin with, nor do they really need any excuse to live the carnal life that they are already likely living. Their *misunderstanding* of the true value of the PreTrib Rapture position simply provides them with an excuse to continue to live carnally. They do not need a push from the PreTrib Rapture doctrine, nor from the person who espouses it.

The PreTrib Rapture doctrine - *if understood correctly* - should prepare people for the fact that at any moment, the Christian will be brought into the Presence of Christ. Those who protest the doctrine of imminency (the belief that Christ *could* come at any moment, because there is nothing that precludes it), seem to be unaware of the big picture (much less the *opinion*).

How Much Longer Will You Live?
How many Christians today actually *live* as if it is their last day on earth? *"Oh, but wait!"* someone might argue. We can argue all we want to about the PreTrib Rapture, the MidTrib, the Absolute Trib, the Pancreatic Trib, or any other trib you would like to argue about. We can then all sit back and rest on our intellectual laurels, once we have tossed out all the "evidence" in favor of our personal position. Then, we can look arrogantly down our nose at the person who just is not spiritually mature enough to see it as we see it. However, what have we accomplished?

How many reading this (who do not believe in a PreTrib Rapture), actually *know* with certainty that life will continue one more day? How many of you reading this do not even consider the fact that you might breathe your last breath before you get to the end of this chapter? That is pretty gloom and doom. Not unless you are dreading to see the face of Jesus Christ in person!

For all these people who think they've got it all figured out, they are really missing the point, because they do not know, nor can they tell, when they are going to die, and head into eternity. No one knows. I may die today, and the Tribulation/Great Tribulation might be 20 years, or 200 years away! I may live another ten years, or 14, or 38 - who knows? Only God knows and He is not telling me. I thank Him for that. Nonetheless, I am *still* required to live *every* day as if it is my *last* day on this earth.

For those who resolutely suppose that believing in the PreTrib Rapture is heresy, because it creates Christians who are immature, lazy, worldly and carnal, the question that must be asked is *do you know when you will die?*

To claim that believing and espousing the PreTrib Rapture creates lazy, spiritual weak, unprepared Christians, is like saying that by teaching that I *could* die today, I am apt to become lazy, immature, carnal, and worldly! It is the *same* thing, folks! If I know there is a chance that I will leave this earth and be taken into His Presence before this day is over, whether by death, or by Rapture, that *will* (or *should*), give me a greater sense of what *is* and what is *not* important! It is as simple as that, and there is NO way to deny it.

Yet, there exists people like Dave MacPherson, and his followers like C. H. Fisher, Tim Warner as well as a multitude of others, who believe beyond doubt that the early church did *not*, under any circumstances, believe or teach an imminent return of Christ - meaning, that His return could happen at any moment. MacPherson is willing to sit in front of a computer, publishing book after book (totaling *eight* to date), on just how wrong the PreTrib Rapture is, and the alleged controversial conspiracy that surrounds it. Nevertheless, do these same folks consider that *today*, their soul might be required of them?

If *all* authentic Christians became more and more aware of the fact that we not only do *not* know *when* we will die, but we are only one breath away from death all the time, then we would have Christians who would have a real and true sense of what is important in this life. We would stop arguing over topics that we cannot know for sure (and that goes for Posttribulationalists and everyone in between, not just PreTrib Rapture people). We would get down to this business, which is the evangelization of the lost, and living a life that glories our Savior and Lord. The Great Commission has *never* been rescinded, yet we live as if it has been. We need to wake up, and live rightly, allowing our lives to witness to the lost. This will only occur when we begin to understand that we are constantly only one breath away from eternity.

I can only imagine what some of those protesting the PreTrib Rapture today, would have said to Noah. *"Hey Noah! Stop the gloom and doom! All your preaching is not changing anyone's mind. We all know you're in it for the notoriety!"* or *"Hey Noah, why are you wasting time building an Ark?! True believers are going to go <u>through</u> the flood, not be saved <u>from</u> it!"*

Christian: we need to understand that God has an agenda and His is the *only* agenda that matters. He is still saving souls, and He is still using His Church to accomplish it, by using Christians to bring the gospel to the lost, in *life*, *word*, and *deed*. The idea that those who believe in the PreTrib Rapture will become spiritually apathetic, immature, and carnal, is simply absurd. Those who continually repeat this charge, simply prove how little they understand, regarding the brevity of life on this planet, including the shortness of their own life.

Chapter 4
You Are Hereby Charged...

To hear the Anti-PreTrib Rapturist tell it, two or three men *re-wrote history*, *lied* about doing so, *plagiarized*, *conspired* to deceive, and generally did all they could to push their own agenda, which was instilling within the average church attendee, belief in the PreTrib Rapture position. If these allegations were not so illogical, they would be comical.

If we take the time to stop and truly *hear* what those who are opposed to the PreTrib Rapture position are actually saying, much of their charges tend toward libel. The problem of course, is that the individuals they are accusing are no longer on this earth, having been taken to the Lord long ago. People who paint C. I. Scofield, or Darby, as wicked men remain safe from having to defend their allegations in the courtroom, because there is no one around today who can sue. Certainly, if Scofield was as much of a scallywag as some indicate, he would not be above dragging people into court, would he?

Tim Warner on the Prowl

As we have seen from quoting Warner previously, it is instantly apparent that Warner has absolutely no patience for Grant Jeffrey (or Thomas Ice, or likely *any* PreTrib Rapturist, because he views them as heretics). This is obvious because of the blanket statements he makes with respect to their views, and *how* he believes they arrived at those views. He, himself, makes some very *bold* claims; claims that border on libel. The reason I say this will become obvious, but in short, they *appear* bold to him, solely *because* of his Posttribulational proclivities. He essentially sees the PreTrib Rapture position, through the eyes of Posttribulationalism. This is not uncommon, and many people do this with Dispensationalism as well. In spite of how charitable they are in presenting their objections[32] to Dispensationalism, they too often present an inaccurate understanding of the very subject with which they are at odds.

In his rebuttal, Warner's opening paragraph states, "*In his 1992 book "Apocalypse," Grant Jeffrey made the astounding claim that some Early Church writers taught an imminent pretribulation rapture. He then selectively quoted several early Christian authors in an attempt to bolster his claim. For many years, posttribulationist authors have quoted these very same authors to illustrate that the early Christians were posttribulationists! Other pretribulationist authors and scholars have*

---

[32] Vern Poythress has done a remarkable job of remaining free of condescension and condemnation in his book, *Understanding Dispensationalism*. However, in the opinion of this author, Poythress presents a number of unintentional inaccuracies regarding normal Dispensationalism. He does so, because he cannot help but see aspects of Dispensationalism through Covenant Theologian glasses.

acknowledged that the early Christians were entirely posttribulation-ists. Grant Jeffrey is the first to my knowledge to make the outrageous claim that the Early Church Fathers taught an imminent pretribulation rapture."[33]

Notice please that Warner makes the statement that *"the early Christians were posttributionist"* and *"pretribulationists authors and scholars have acknowledged that the early Christians were entirely posttribulationists."* It would have been nice if Warner had offered something in the way of support for his statements. In fact, the foot-notes he *does* include, leaves something to be desired, because they do not provide a conclusive statement regarding from which of Jeffrey's books he quotes for instance, merely listing the reference as *Apocalypse*. Since Jeffrey has two books with the word "Apocalypse" in the title, unless someone has both books, it will prove difficult to determine. Neither of the books – *Apocalypse: The Coming Judgment,* or *Countdown to the Apocalypse* – have a publication date of 1992 as Warner lists. If I had to guess, I would say Warner is quoting from the first book, which has a publication date of 1994, 1995, and 1997. It is possible that an edition of it *was* published in 1992, as Warner states, however a 1992 edition could not be located, nor other refer-ences to it.

Liar, Liar, Pants on Fire!
Referring to Jeffrey's statements regarding the early church teaching the imminent return of Christ, Warner rebuts him with, *"None of the early Christian writers indicated a belief in an imminent pretribulation rapture. There is no evidence whatever of a debate in the early Church regarding the timing of the rapture! Posttribulationism was the only rapture view espoused by any of the writers of the Ante-Nicene period (from the Apostles until the council of Nicea in 325AD)."*[34]

---

[33] http://www.oasischristianchurch.org/air/Jeffrey.pdf
[34] http://www.oasischristianchurch.org/air/Jeffrey.pdf

This is a difficult statement to make, yet Warner has no difficulty making it. Whenever anyone makes this type of statement with respect to Eschatology, a red flag goes up in my mind. It is one thing to come to a specific conclusion regarding *aspects* of Eschatology. However, when someone comes across with such haughtiness, it is normally due to his or her own overworked ego.

As previously noted, one of the main reasons the church fathers were somewhat ambiguous concerning the End Times events, was because that they were far more concerned about doctrines like the deity of Christ, the Triune nature of the Godhead, salvation by grace alone, or by grace and works, as well as other areas. These important topics would be dealt with before a doctrine such as imminence, or other areas of Eschatology. Of course, we cannot forget the backdrop of their lives, which was generally turmoil, depending upon where they lived, and who ruled. It was a tenuous situation at best.

One needs only to peruse the halls of church history to understand the type of error that the Church battled against well into the third century and beyond. It is unbelievable to consider the amount of error that made headway into the Church, even while Paul was alive (cf. Galatians). These errors went from stating that Christ had not really come in the flesh, to the fact that Jesus was not God, and plenty in between.

Imminence Again...
It seems clear enough that Peter, John and Paul and the other apostles expected Christ to return during their lifetime, or at least during their generation. Peter himself said, "*For the culmination of all things is near. So be self-controlled and sober-minded for the sake of prayer. Above all keep your love for one another fervent, because love covers a multitude of sins,*" (1 Peter 4:7-8 NET).

The apostle John, stated, *"Children, it is the last hour, and just as you heard that the antichrist is coming, so now many antichrists have appeared. We know from this that it is the last hour,"* (1 John 2:18 NET).

Paul stated in Romans, *"And do this because we know the time, that it is already the hour for us to awake from sleep, for our salvation is now nearer than when we became believers. The night has advanced toward dawn; the day is near. So then we must lay aside the works of darkness, and put on the weapons of light,"* (Romans 13:11-12 NET).

1 Thessalonians

But consider 1 Thessalonians. Paul has spent the first three chapters of 1 Thessalonians pointing out the fact of the quality of faith exhibited by the Thessalonian believers. In chapter three, he reminds them of the time that he had spent with them, working hard to proclaim and live the gospel of Jesus Christ, so that good fruit would be seen in the lives of the Thessalonians. Paul states how much he wanted to see them again, but could not. He sent Timothy, because he wanted to be sure that none of his work had been in vain. The first letter to the Thessalonians was written *after* Timothy had been able to report to Paul, from his visit with the Thessalonians.

Timothy not only came back with a good report, related to how the Thessalonian believers were doing, but he also came back with at least one question that he was unable to answer for them. He relayed the question to Paul, and we see his response to their query toward the end of chapter four (vv. 13-18). He states,

"But we do not want you to be uninformed, brothers, about those who are asleep, that you may not grieve as others do who have no hope. For since we believe that Jesus died and rose again, even so, through Jesus, God will bring with him those who have fallen asleep. For this we declare to you by a word from the Lord, that we who are alive, who are left until the coming of the Lord, will not precede those who have fallen asleep. For the Lord himself will descend from heaven with a cry of com-

mand, with the voice of an archangel, and with the sound of the trumpet of God. And the dead in Christ will rise first. Then we who are alive, who are left, will be caught up together with them in the clouds to meet the Lord in the air, and so we will always be with the Lord. Therefore encourage one another with these words."

If we consider what Paul is stating here, it is difficult to believe that he is speaking of the Second Coming *following* the Great Tribulation. If that were the case, would it *not* have been beneficial for Paul to say something about this upcoming horrific period of time, which serves to close human history? Instead, we see Paul encouraging the Thessalonians not to "grieve." The Thessalonian believers were not like the pagans, who had no hope. They already *knew* that those who were dead in Christ would rise to be with Him forever. They were concerned about those who had died since Paul had been with them. Were they going to miss being "caught up" to the Lord?

Paul is encouraging them (v. 18), to keep looking up, in essence. He is reminding them that those who have died in Christ will actually be raised to life incorruptible *prior* to those believers who remained alive. If Paul was speaking of a resurrection that took place *after* the Tribulation/Great Tribulation period, his whole line of thought here would not really make sense. In fact, would not the Thessalonian believers actually be *relieved* that instead of having to experience the worst seven years this planet will ever see, a number of believers they knew and loved, had already *died*, which meant of course, that they would miss the terrible period altogether? Why on earth would the Thessalonian believers be grieving for people who had already died, never having to experience the Tribulation/Great Tribulation period, if that is what they had to look forward to?! Would they not be glad that these believers had been spared the experience, by being taken to the Lord beforehand?

The following verses in chapter five of 1 Thessalonians continue to bring the point home. Paul states, *"Now concerning the times and the seasons, brothers, you have no need to have anything written to you. For you yourselves are fully aware that the day of the Lord will come like a thief in the night. While people are saying, 'There is peace and security,' then sudden destruction will come upon them as labor pains come upon a pregnant woman, and they will not escape,"* (1 Thessalonians 5:1-3).

Peace and Safety During the Tribulation? Huh?

It is equally difficult to believe that there will be a time during the Tribulation/Great Tribulation that will *appear* to be one of peace and safety. All one has to do is study the sections of Scripture which deal specifically with the Tribulation/Great Tribulation period (cf. Revelation 6-19:21, as just one example).

The Tribulation begins, with the Lamb, Himself, opening the first of seven Seals. The entire seven-year period is God-ordained, and *from* God's hand, (cf. Revelation 6:1-8:5):

- *Antichrist*
- *War and Bloodshed*
- *Pestilence and Death*
- *Martyrs*
- *Great earthquake*
- *30 minutes of silence/Golden Censer*

Do you see peace and safety in any of the above? If we move to the next part of the Tribulation, we encounter the Seven Trumpets (cf. Revelation 8:7-11:19):

- *Hail, fire, blood*
- *Burning mountain*
- *Star – wormwood*
- *Sun diminished*
- *Plague of locusts (first woe)*
- *Plague of horsemen (second woe)*

- *Reference to Christ ruling*

Again, is there anything here that indicates peace and safety? The next part highlights seven key figures (cf. Revelation 12:1-13:18):

- *Woman – Israel*
- *Dragon – Satan*
- *Male Child – Christ*
- *Michael – the Archangel*
- *Remnant – Saved Israel*
- *Antichrist – Beast out of the sea*
- *False prophet – beast out of the earth*

The above noted figures are briefly summarized in this section of Revelation. The Tribulation has now gotten to the halfway point and moves into the *Great* Tribulation period. It is at this point, where the Antichrist breaks his covenant with Israel, and begins to persecute the Jews. Here we see the following occur (cf. Revelation 15:1-16:21), beginning with the seven bowls:

- *Boils*
- *Sea turns to blood*
- *Rivers to blood*
- *Great heat*
- *Darkness*
- *Euphrates dried up*
- *Hail*

Peace and safety still seems not to be apparent in any of the above bulleted areas. In fact, it certainly seems to be worsening.

The next aspect of the Great Tribulation highlights seven things, which occur on Babylon (cf. Revelation 17:1-18:24):

- *Devoid of human life*

- *Burned with fire*
- *Destroyed in one hour*
- *People afraid to enter her borders*
- *Riches brought to nothing*
- *Violently overthrown*
- *All activity ceases*

Yet again, we see no reason to think that there is peace and safety during this time of the Great Tribulation. The very last aspect of the Great Tribulation climaxes with the return of Jesus Christ with His saints. During this time, a number of events take place (cf. Revelation 19:1-21):

- *Battle of Armageddon*
- *Marriage of the Lamb*
- *Return of Christ with the Church and His angels*
- *Antichrist and False Prophet cast into the Lake of Fire[35]*

Paul specifically tells the Thessalonians, "*While people are saying, 'There is peace and security,' then sudden destruction will come upon them as labor pains come upon a pregnant woman, and they will not escape.*" Paul is obviously teaching that there will be a time when people *will* believe that peace and safety has finally come to earth! There is no place in all of the Tribulation/Great Tribulation period where this can be true, so Paul, of necessity, *must* be speaking of a time *prior* to the Tribulation/Great Tribulation, which will lead *up to* Israel's signing of the seven-year covenant, with the Antichrist. Paul cannot be speaking of a time at the *end* of the Great Tribulation either, because that is going to be the final showdown and climax!

Will His Second Coming Be Like a Thief?

How can His day *come as a thief* if people will have the ability to

---

[35] Information related to the Tribulation/Great Tribulation taken from *Charting the End Times*, by Tim LaHaye and Thomas Ice (Eugene Harvest House 2001), 57

count down from the start of the Tribulation/Great Tribulation, seven years, or 2,520 days (1,260 x 2)? Who would *not* be able to do this? Figuring out Jesus' Second Coming (almost to the day), would not be that difficult at all, as long as the *starting* point of the Tribulation is *known*.

We need to remember that *if* the Rapture occurs prior to the start of the Tribulation/Great Tribulation, there are no signs that point to that coming event, as to the day *or* the hour. This is not true of His Second Coming, which ushers in the end of the Great Tribulation, as pointed out above.

We also need to remember that should the Rapture occur prior to the start of the Tribulation, there will be many left on earth that *had* been churchgoers. They had *heard* the gospel many times, and may have even *thought* they were Christians. It will only be when the Rapture occurs, and they are not participants, that they will come to terms with the fact that they have *never* received Christ as Savior.

Some accuse that the PreTrib Rapture position gives people a "second chance." However, the truth is that as long as people are *alive,* they will always have a chance to receive Christ. Throughout a person's lifetime, they will be given as many chances by God as they need to receive His salvation.

Those who are not taken in the Rapture are *not dead.* They are very much alive, and facing an atmosphere on earth like none before it! There will come a point during the Great Tribulation when people will have to make a decision whether or not to receive the mark of the beast. If they succumb and take the mark, they will at that point, be giving up all chances for salvation. They will have sold their souls to Satan (cf. Revelation 14:9).

I believe both Jesus and Paul are referring to a situation *prior* to the start of the Tribulation. There will come a time when it *appears* as though peace and safety has finally come to earth, but this is merely a deceptive cover, briefly hiding the most horrible time this world will have ever seen. It is difficult to understand how people can see not see a time of alleged peace *before* the Tribulation/Great Tribulation, but that is what Posttribulationists do, as well as others. It seems obvious that in order for Israel to *want* to enter into a covenant with Antichrist, she will *believe* that peace and safety is within reach.

Christ's "Two" Second Comings

Regarding Christ's Second Coming, it is not *two* Second Comings, or two phases of His Second Coming. Of the actual Second Coming of Christ, there is only *one event* and it occurs at the *end* of the Great Tribulation. With the Rapture, the Lord does *not* return to this earth, and it takes place *prior* to, and separately from, the Second Coming.

The two events are not directly connected. It is much like the illustration titled "**Are There Two Second Comings?**" on the next page. The top portion of the figure shows a dad, standing in the open front door of the house, calling for his kids to come home for dinner. The dad *never* leaves the house. He has simply stepped to the front porch, having opened the door, and calls to his children to come home, from there.

The bottom half of the illustration shows that the dad has gone to the park *with* his child. He actually left the house, and walked with his son to the park for some catch, or some other activity.

The two events are *different* and *not related*. The only way they are related is in the fact that when the PreTrib Rapture occurs, it will be known that the start of the Tribulation is not that far away.

What is also interesting to consider is the fact that *if* the PreTrib Rapture is legitimately taught in the Bible and *does* occur prior to the start of the Tribulation, consider what this world will look like immediately afterwards. There will be quite a mess following the Rapture. Consider 20 million people, or more, suddenly vanishing off the planet. Allow your mind to picture what that will look like. It will cause so much chaos, that the world will desperately need someone to lead them through this crisis. Someone will need to step up to calm nerves, and present a plan to put things back in order. This is the perfect opportunity for the Antichrist to make his presence known. The world will need a leader and they will get one.

Tim Warner sees it differently, regarding the early church. *"The only eschatological debate that developed concerned the Millennium, and whether the blessings associated with it were to be literally understood. The early Christians believed in a future, literal 70th week, a literal Antichrist, and a single coming of Jesus after the tribulation to raise the dead saints, rapture the living saints, and destroy the Antichrist. [Grant] Jeffrey boldly manipulated these authors in an attempt to portray them as pretribulationists. His treatment of this issue is the most blatant pretribulationist revisionism I have ever seen."*[36]

What? No Evidence?
Again, Warner fails to provide any evidence (convincing or otherwise), in support of his declarative statements. Apparently, he assumes that his references to beliefs held by the early church writers (whoever they may be), is generally accepted knowledge, that does not require documented support.

However, Warner is not finished. He also takes issue with Grant Jeffrey's partial quote of the Didache (otherwise known as the *Teaching of the Twelve Apostles*). Here is Jeffrey's quote from Section 16 of the Didache:

---

[36] Ibid

"'1 Be ye watchful for your life! Let not your lamps be extinguished, nor your loins ungirded, but be ye ready! For ye know not the hour in which your Lord cometh.

2. Assemble yourselves frequently, seeking what is fitting for your souls. For the whole time of your faith will not be profitable to you, if you are not made perfect in the last time...then the world deceiver shall appear as a son of god and shall work signs and wonders...

6. And then shall the signs of the truth appear, first the sign of a rift in heaven; then the sign of the sound of a trumpet, and the thirdly, a resurrection of the dead.

7. But not of all, but as it was said, 'The Lord will come and all His saints with Him.

8. Then shall the world see the Lord coming upon the clouds of heaven.'...'

After warning Christians to prepare for "the hour in which your Lord cometh," the Didache said, "Then, the world-deceiver shall appear." This order of events suggests the Rapture will precede the appearance of the world-deceiver, the Antichrist."[37]

Please note that it is obvious (from the numbering), that Jeffrey *skipped* portions of the Didache. If he was *deliberately* attempting to deceive, it is doubtful he would have included numbers at all. Warner though, comments on it by stating, "*In Jeffrey's truncated version of the Didache, and his analysis of it, the illusion of a secret rapture is developed from the exhortation to "watch" for the coming of the Lord (if one supposes, as Jeffrey does, that "watching" automatically implies an any-moment advent). Jeffrey points out that the "watching" is prior to*

---

[37] http://www.oasischristianchurch.org/air/Jeffrey.pdf

the appearance of Antichrist, and so infers a pretribulation rapture, even though the passage never mentions a pretribulation coming."[38]

The Same Translation Would Have Been Good

Warner then quotes what Jeffrey quoted, including the omitted parts. However, it should be pointed out that Warner, for some reason, chose to quote from a completely *different* translation of the Didache, than did Jeffrey:

> "*Watch for your life's sake. Let not your lamps be quenched, nor your loins unloosed; but be ye ready, for ye know not the hour in which our Lord cometh. But often shall ye come together, seeking the things which are befitting to your souls: for the whole time of your faith will not profit you, if ye be not made perfect in the last time.* **For in the last days false prophets and corrupters shall be multiplied, and the sheep shall be turned into wolves, and love shall be turned into hate; for when lawlessness increaseth, they shall hate and persecute and betray one another,** *and then shall appear the world-deceiver as Son of God, and shall do signs and wonders,* **and the earth shall be delivered into his hands, and he shall do iniquitous things which have never yet come to pass since the beginning. Then shall the creation of men come into the fire of trial, and many shall be made to stumble and shall perish; but they that endure in their faith shall be saved from under the curse itself.** *And then shall appear the signs of the truth; first, the sign of an out-spreading in heaven; then the sign of the sound of the trumpet; and the third, the resurrection of the dead; yet not of all, but as it is said: The Lord shall come and all His saints with Him. Then shall the world see the Lord coming upon the clouds of heaven.*"[39]

---

[38] http://www.oasischristianchurch.org/air/Jeffrey.pdf
[39] Ibid

The bolded sections are the ones that Warner included (which are in red type in his document). As near as I can tell, Warner used the version of the Didache found on the New Advent website.[40] However, Warner could also have used the Didache translation by Roberts-Donaldson.[41] It is simply not clear.

Revisionism?

The main point of Warner's protest is that he firmly believes that Jeffrey is guilty of *deception* through *revisionism*. The truth though seems to be in Jeffrey's corner because of the overwhelming biblical evidence that the early Church believed in an imminent return of Christ.

In noting the last section of the Didache, it states "*the resurrection of the dead; **yet not of all**, but as it is said: The Lord shall come and all His saints with Him.*" Please note that an apparent resurrection has already occurred, noted by the words "yet not of all." Some have already been resurrected and are already *with* the Lord at His return.

The Didache and the Olivet Discourse

I would agree that much of this portion of the Didache is reminiscent of the Olivet Discourse. While I believe Jesus is speaking mainly to Jewish individuals, as His mission was to seek and save the lost of the household of Israel (cf. Matthew 15:24; Luke 19:9). Because of that, it is clear that Jesus was outlining the events of the End Times, as they *primarily related to Israel*. Since He was speaking *to* Jewish people, He was explaining what would happen *with* and *to* them during the Last Days, leading up to, and including the Tribulation/Great Tribulation.

I believe Jeffrey is also correct by the *inference* within the Didache. If in fact, Jesus was speaking to, and about the nation of Israel, then He is *not* speaking *to*, or *about* the Church. There can only be one reason

---

[40] http://www.newadvent.org/fathers/0714.htm
[41] http://www.earlychristianwritings.com/text/didache-roberts.html

that He is not speaking to or about the Church, and that is because the Church has been raptured off the planet. The part where Christ begins discussing the Rapture begins with verse 36 of Matthew 24.

Before we deal with the Rapture in this section of Scripture, let us continue with Warner and his critique of Jeffrey's comments. He states,

> "The [Didache] author's paraphrase of Matthew 24:9-15 shows that he was following the Olivet Discourse. And this quote from which Jeffrey derives his pretribulation rapture comes from the same passage. Jesus said, **"but of that day and hour knows no man"** (Matt. 24:36). The question is, WHAT "day or hour" was Jesus (and the Didache) referring to? The answer is found in verses 29-31, "immediately after the tribulation ... they shall see the Son of Man coming in the clouds of heaven with power and great glory." Jesus clearly had His posttribulation coming in view when He said that no one knows the "day or hour." So, when the author of the Didache quoted these words, there is no reason to assume that he meant something other than what Jesus said! Jeffrey **interpreted** these words of Jesus as modern pretribulationists do, rather than in their context. By injecting the modern pretribulationist concept of "any moment" imminence into this statement, and omitting the parts that expose his scheme, Jeffrey was able to give an illusion of a pretribulation rapture."[42] (emphasis added)

I will respectfully take issue with Warner's understanding of the phrase *"but of that day and hour knows no man."* While it is noteworthy, that Warner indicated that Jeffrey *interpreted* the words of the Didache (as opposed to *changing* or *revising* them); it would appear as though Warner himself is interpreting the Didache, based solely on his partiality for Posttribulationism.

---

[42] http://www.oasischristianchurch.org/air/Jeffrey.pdf

It's the Rapture

By the time Jesus has gotten to verse 36, of Matthew 24, He is just beginning a new section. Let me quote from Arnold Fruchtenbaum here, which should clarify this for us.

> "...Matthew 24:36 begins with the word But, which in Greek is peri de. The peri de construction in Greek is **a contrastive introduction of a new subject** and, hence, is often translated as: But concerning (1 Cor. 7:1; 8:1; 12:1; 16:1; 1 Thess 5:1; etc.). **The usage of this construction points to the introduction of a new subject.** So yes, He has been discussing the Second Coming until this point. However, the peri de means that He is now introducing a new subject, and that is the Rapture. This would not be the first time the chronological sequence of the Olivet Discourse was broken to speak of an earlier event. It also happened in Luke 21:12. In answer to the second point, in Greek, the 'taking away' in verses 40-41 is a different Greek word than the one used in verse 39, and so it need not be interpreted as the same kind of 'taking away'."[43] (emphasis added)

One has to wonder why Warner himself did not take the time to delve into the original languages. However, since Warner is a Post-tribulationist, then to him, it only makes sense that the Rapture will happen *at the moment, or just prior to,* the Lord's Second Coming. This is why Warner can see nothing related to the Rapture within the context of the Olivet Discourse, but sees it as referencing only the Tribulation/Great Tribulation and the Lord's Second Coming (which incorporates the Rapture, for Posttribulationalism).

This may be too simple, but consider this: If we know that the Tribulation/Great Tribulation *begins* with the signing of the covenant (as delineated in Daniel 9:27, where the last "week" of the 70 weeks is defined), would it not be possible to simply *count down* from that

---

[43] Arnold G. Fruchtenbaum *Footsteps of the Messiah* (San Antonio: Ariel 2003), 641

point, to learn and know *when* Jesus would actually be returning? If it can be figured out *when* He will be returning, then Jesus' comment regarding no one knowing the day or the hour must be referring to something else. If His comment was referring to something else, it could only have been referring to the Rapture of the Church, prior to the beginning of the Tribulation/Great Tribulation period.

Let us look at the actual text here from Matthew:

> *"But concerning that day and hour no one knows, not even the angels of heaven, nor the Son, but the Father only. For as were the days of Noah, so will be the coming of the Son of Man. For as in those days before the flood they were eating and drinking, marrying and giving in marriage, until the day when Noah entered the ark, and they were unaware until the flood came and swept them all away, so will be the coming of the Son of Man. Then two men will be in the field; one will be taken and one left. Two women will be grinding at the mill; one will be taken and one left. Therefore, stay awake, for you do not know on what day your Lord is coming. But know this, that if the master of the house had known in what part of the night the thief was coming, he would have stayed awake and would not have let his house be broken into. Therefore you also must be ready, for the Son of Man is coming at an hour you do not expect,"* (Matthew 25:36-44).

Warner Goes Backwards; Christ Goes Forward
Regarding the Matthew passage, Warner goes *back* to verses 29-31 for the answer to *"but of the day and hour..."* My question is *why did he do that?* It appears to me that Jesus, in verse 35 of Matthew 24, has just finished detailing the coming days, which will ultimately culminate in His return.

As noted, beginning in verse 36, Jesus begins a new (albeit somewhat related), section, connecting the End Times with those of Noah's day. If we consider the text in Matthew, Jesus says that the very end of human history will be very much like it was in the days of Noah. We know from Genesis 6:8, that Noah had found favor in God's eyes. Because of this favored status, God reveals to him that He is going to destroy the world with a global flood. Everyone will die, except Noah, his family and some animals.

Fruchtenbaum rightly points out that,

> *"When the Rapture occurs, it will happen while there are normal conditions on the earth. The Flood also came while there were normal conditions on the earth, while men were eating, and drinking, marrying and giving in marriage. None of these things are sinful, but are necessary for human survival and propagation. While normal conditions existed on earth, the Noahic Flood arrived and swept them all away. In the same way, while there are normal conditions on the earth, the Rapture will suddenly*

occur, sweeping away all believers (vv. 40-41). This will not be true of the Second Coming. When that event occurs, conditions on earth will be far from normal, as earlier sections of the Olivet Discourse and the Book of Revelation clearly show."[44]

God tells Noah to begin building an Ark, and Noah does as he is told. For the next 120 years or so (cf. Genesis 6:3b), Noah not only built an Ark, but also preached to the people about the coming judgment of God. Finally, it was time to enter into the Ark. This Noah did, with the animals that God brought to him. Therefore, Noah and his family, and all the animals were safely shut into the Ark, (cf. Genesis 7:16).

By the way, as a bit of an aside here, please note that the narrative jumps around a bit in Genesis 7:1-24. Here is how it would look if we outlined it:

> *Please note that as He did with Abram, God told Noah to build an Ark. Noah did as God ordered. This was not a covenant. It was a directive, exactly what it was with Abram.*

- God tells Noah to enter the Ark, with the animals. Noah does (Genesis 7:1-5).
- We read of Noah's age, and a repeat of Noah entering the Ark, with the animals (Genesis 7:6-10).
- We read of Noah's age again; the rain began and continued for 40 days and 40 nights; that day, Noah and his family entered the Ark; the Lord shuts the Ark up from the outside (Genesis 7:11-16).

---

[44] Arnold G. Fruchtenbaum *Footsteps of the Messiah* (San Antonio: Ariel 2003), 641-42

- Rains continued for 40 days and 40 nights; Ark floated on top of the waters; the water was so high that they covered the highest mountains by 15 cubits; all living outside the Ark died; waters prevailed for 150 days (Genesis 7:17-24).

As we can see from the above, details were provided, but often, the same details were repeated and/or expanded upon. This happens often throughout the Bible, yet Warner seems to either not notice it as it occurs in the Matthew 24 passage, or he ignores it altogether.

The Upcoming Flood

What we see with Noah, is God warning him of the upcoming flood. Noah prepares for that day by building the Ark and preaching to the people on earth, who will unfortunately, be killed in the upcoming global flood. Once everything has been established and God's timetable had arrived, He told Noah to enter the Ark. Once Noah, his family, and the animals were safe in the Ark, God seals it up from outside. It is *after* this, that the global flood begins, which is understood as God's wrath being poured out onto the earth and all who dwell in it. God's purpose at this point was destruction of rebels.

During the torrential downpour, the "fountains of the deep" also opened up and literally engulfed the world with water. However, Noah and all within the Ark were completely safe. The Posttribulationist would say that Noah and the rest were kept safe *during and within* the wrath that was poured out in the form of the global flood. In my view, it appears to be more accurate to say that Noah and the rest were completely *removed* from the floodwaters. They experienced *none* of it, as none of it touched them. They were safely tucked away *inside* the Ark, with plenty of food, water, and comfort. There was no other place for God to place them unless He removed them to heaven. However, obviously, in order for that to occur, He would also have to change their bodies to meet the conditions and environment of heaven. Since God needed Noah and his sons to re-populate the earth, He needed to keep them on the earth, but *away* from the reach of His wrath, via the Flood, which destroyed everything else on the face of the earth.

This is *not* the way the Tribulation/Great Tribulation is depicted for any of the "saints" that go through it. The only exception is His Remnant, which He supernaturally saves and provides for, during a specific time of the Tribulation/Great Tribulation.

It is clear to me at least, that Noah, his family, and the animals were safely *removed* from the dangers of the upcoming global flood, *before* it even *started* raining. Noah was not given the knowledge of the "day or hour" in which God would tell him to go into the Ark, nor was He given advance notice about *when* God would begin pouring out His wrath, *until* He told Noah to enter the Ark (cf. Genesis 7:4).

Noah Did Not Know the Day or Hour Until God Told Him
The point is simple to explain, and should be just as simple to grasp. Noah was not told *when* the floodwaters would *start*. He was unaware of the day or the hour God's wrath would begin to be poured out on humanity. Noah did not need to know it, *until* he needed to know it.

Christ Himself points to Noah. Warner apparently missed that completely, preferring to go *back* to verses 29-31 of Matthew 24. His very last comment on Jeffrey's opinion is, "*By injecting the modern pretribulationist concept of "any moment" imminence into this statement, and omitting the parts that expose his scheme, Jeffrey was able to give an illusion of a pretribulation rapture.*" Warner then moves on to deal with *The Epistle of Barnabas*. He does not refer to Noah's day at all. Why? Because when Noah's day is considered, it is difficult not to understand that Noah, et al, were safely taken *out of the way* even before God sent the rain. If this does not refer to a type of PreTrib Rapture, then what does? In this author's opinion, Jesus says quite a bit by referring to the days of Noah at that point in His Olivet sermon. He says essentially "*For as in those days before the flood they were eating and drinking, marrying and giving in marriage, until the day when Noah entered the ark, and they were unaware until the flood came and swept them all away, so will be the coming of the Son of Man,"* (Matthew 24:38-39).

Immediately following that section of Scripture containing information on the Rapture, Christ presents a number of parables, which point to the time *after* the Tribulation/Great Tribulation. This first parable begins in Matthew 24:45 through 51, and is generally known as some form of the Faithful Servant. Here, we see that there is *work* involved in being a Christian, not simply *watching*. Fruchtenbaum comments, "*The emphasis of [the Faithful Servant] parable is on* laboring. *In order to make sure that the believers do not misconstrue the previous emphasis on watching as meaning, 'just to sit there and look at the sky,' [this] parable emphasizes the necessity of working while one is waiting. When the Messiah returns, it will be while believers are busy laboring. The believer will be found laboring, but the unbeliever will be found not laboring.*"[45]

Christ continues with the parable of the ten virgins (cf. Matthew 24:1-13), the parable of the talents (cf. Matthew 24:14-30), and the time of judgment (cf. Matthew 24:31-46). Each of these emphasizes a different aspect of being prepared, watching for the Lord, and working *while* watching. The judgment of the Gentiles is where the application of the parables comes together. Fruchtenbaum sheds light on this.

> "*The* time *of the judgment will be after the Second Coming...(v. 31). The* place *of the judgment is not given in this passage, but it is given in a parallel passage found in Joel 31-3...the subjects of the judgment are individuals; this will be an individual judgment rather than a national one (vv. 32-33). The Greek word trans-lated* nations *has the primary meaning of 'Gentiles' and is so*

---

[45] Arnold G. Fruchtenbaum *Footsteps of the Messiah* (San Antonio: Ariel 2003), 644

translated elsewhere in the New Testament. All the Gentiles who survive the Tribulation and the Campaign of Armageddon will be gathered into the Valley of Jehoshaphat and will then be separated by the Messiah; some are brought to His left side and some are brought to His right side. Those brought to His right are called the sheep *Gentiles, and those brought to His left are called the* goat *Gentiles.*

"The basis of this judgment is going to be anti-Semitism or pro-Semitism. The individual Gentiles will be judged on the basis of their treatment of the Messiah's brethren, *namely, the Jewish people during the Tribulation (vv. 34-35). Some have tried to make the term* brethren *refer to saints in general, but this would render the passage meaningless. There are three specific groups mentioned in this passage: the* sheep *Gentiles, the* goat *Gentiles, and the* brethren. *If the* brethren *are saints in general, then who are the* sheep, *since they, too, have eternal life? It would be very confusing to make both the* sheep *and the* brethren *as* saints *of the same caliber. From this context alone, it should be very evident that the* brethren *must refer to Jewish people because the saints are the* sheep *and the unsaved are the* goats. *Furthermore, the parallel passage of Joel 3:1-3 makes it certain that these* brethren *are the Jewish people of the Tribulation."*[46]

Fruchtenbaum then comments on the passage that the sheep are the righteous, while the goats are the unrighteous, both receiving their designation from the way they individually treated Jewish people. Each individual was found to be anti-Semitic, or pro-Semitic, and His judgment was based on this. This should serve as a strong warning against anti-Semitism, yet it is becoming once again, all too prevalent in today's society.

---

[46] Arnold G. Fruchtenbaum *Footsteps of the Messiah* (San Antonio: Ariel 2003), 648

A Misunderstanding of Concepts

This whole problem that Warner's attitude manifests against Jeffrey, reminds me of those who criticize and review Dispensationalism. They normally do so by placing the *template* of their own beliefs on top of Dispensationalism, and then they begin to review it. The problem in the situation with respect to Jeffrey and Warner is that Warner sees the Church as being on earth during the Tribulation/Great Tribulation. He does so because he sees absolutely no difference between the "Church" in the Old Testament and the Church in the New Testament. In spite of the fact that Paul explains the *mystery* of the Church, which had not been revealed prior to his revealing it, Warner disagrees with Paul. Warner would say that the Church is actually referenced in the OT, and believes this because the word *ekklesia* is used in the OT. His reasoning then, is that since this word was used in the OT, it must be referring to the Church. This is hindsight reasoning. He is interpolating knowledge of the NT Church, and looking *backwards* to the OT to find references of it.

As already noted, just because the word *ekklesia* was used in the OT to signify a *gathering together*, or a *congregation*, this is not proof that the word was being used to represent *the* Church. In fact, it is *much more* likely that the word was *adopted* for the Church, since it was already in common usage. What also needs to be understood is that the original Hebrew word in the OT is translated church in English, however, this does not necessarily tell the full story. A word *and* context study needs to be employed to gain full access to the meaning, as we have discussed.

Words with Multiple Meanings

The word *church* can mean the following:

1. *The visible Church*
2. *The invisible Church*
3. *A building in which people meet for worship*

It is only through the context, is it understood which particular meaning the word "church" is referencing. To say that the word "church" means the exact same thing in every usage would be incorrect.

One other example is the word *mean*. This word also has more than one definition:

1. *Average (as in math-related computations)*
2. *Spiteful*
3. *Miserly*

Here again, the context would come into play in determining which definition was applicable.

We call these types of words *homonyms*, and we do so for a reason. If an advertisement states "Let's Spring into Spring!", we would understand the first usage of "spring" to refer to an action, while the second usage of the word "spring" refers to the time of year, or season.

So unfortunately, Warner, in condemning Jeffrey, is actually using his own (Warner's) definition for his understanding of what the "church" is, and to him, Jesus is speaking to *all* the saints, which applies to the "Church," even though other passages of Scripture seem to clearly indicate that the invisible Church is gone. It is because Warner is a Posttribulationist that he makes no distinction between the "saints" of the OT and the Church of the NT.

Does the Posttribulationalist or the PreTrib Rapturist have a more valid argument?

Chapter 5
It Came from the Pit!

The PreTrib Rapture position, unlike any other Rapture position held, is seen by an increasing number of people as not only deceptive, but a deception that comes straight from the pit of hell. This is tragic. Aside from this, does it not seem strange that it is *only* the PreTrib Rapture viewpoint that is coming under such tremendous fire? It is odd, to say the least, however, in the end, maybe it is not that odd.

From the perspective of those who do not agree with the PreTrib Rapture position, the major argument is that it is seen as something that lets people off the hook, so to speak, or an provides escape hatch/clause. It could be asked, why would any Christian seriously consider *not* wanting to suffer for Christ? After all, did He not suffer to death for *us*? Of course He did and no one who understands what Christianity is all about would deny that.

However, this viewpoint that the PreTrib Rapture position is deceptive and born in hell seems to ignore some very logical points regarding the nature of the Church and those who make up the Church, upon receiving their salvation. It is almost as if, though people understand that they become Christians based solely on the work of Christ, they somehow feel that they must *maintain* their Christianity in their own strength, on their own, through their own individual work. This completely leaves Christ out of the picture, and does not even consider the seal of the Holy Spirit and His constant indwelling.

A visit to Tim Warner's church website sheds light on this. As mentioned, the church he pastors makes the following statement with respect to salvation:

> *"Salvation - God is ready, willing, and able to save and declare righteous anyone who obeys the Gospel. Jesus is drawing all people by His Spirit to repentance. But, most resist Him and will perish. Obeying the Gospel means hearing and understanding the Gospel, believing the message of the Gospel, turning from sin (repentance) to Christ, and being baptized unto Christ upon one's confession that "Jesus is the Christ the Son of God." Baptism itself does not save. God alone saves. Baptism is the normal act of obedience to the Gospel. When someone obeys the Gospel, God forgives and sets them free from sins, adopts them into His family, renovates the heart, and baptizes them with His Spirit. **Continuing in faith in Christ until the end of life is necessary for our salvation to be permanent.** Salvation is of the whole person,*

*spirit, soul, and body. The completion of our salvation awaits the
resurrection of the body "at His coming."*[47]

A Real Lack of Security

The reader will observe that Warner's view of salvation *precludes*
any security. While it might appear as though Warner's comments
are *spiritual* in nature, they are actually anti-spiritual, in that the individual is required to *work* or *earn* salvation; something that Paul
spent the entirety of his epistle to the Galatian churches correcting
them about. What Christ begins, according to Warner's understanding of salvation, the Christian must *finish*. Disagreements over eternal security, and whether the authentic Christian can actually lose
salvation, have existed for some time. Certainly, that debate is not
going to be solved in this book.

The real tragedy though, is that while Paul makes things absolutely
clear with respect to the fact that no one can *earn* salvation (cf. Galatians; Ephesians 2), there are obviously those who continue to believe that this is not what Paul actually meant at all. The Roman
Catholic Church immediately comes to mind, with their many *addi-
tions* to salvation by grace alone. Whether it is baptism, the Euchar-
ist, confession, penance, or something else placed upon the shoulders
of the believer, those are fabricated requirements, which are added
to the gospel of grace. Since these requirements are fabricated, and
done through man's own efforts, they cannot *affect* salvation for the
individual, and they stand at odds with the free gift of eternal life.

Warner's church seems to say the same thing. Their statement in-
tones that it is obedience to the gospel (which is defined as "*hearing
and understanding the Gospel, believing the message of the Gospel,
turning from sin (repentance) to Christ, and being baptized unto Christ
upon one's confession that "Jesus is the Christ the Son of God."* This is

---

[47] http://www.oasischristianchurch.org/beliefs.html

nothing more than a *program* that one places their faith *in*, as opposed to the One in whom faith should be placed.

Though Warner states that baptism does not actually save anyone, it would appear though, that without it, the believer is not actually *obeying* the Gospel, according to that statement of belief. It also appears plain that, without obedience, Warner is teaching that there is no salvation, in spite of his statement to the contrary. The entire *emphasis* found within their definition of *salvation,* is duly placed on the *individual* Christian. There is nothing in their verbiage, which states that Christ is the *Author* as well as the *Perfecter* of our faith, (cf. Hebrews 12:2). In fact, it appears as if Jesus is nearly completely removed from the equation! There is no mention of the indwelling and *empowering* of the Holy Spirit either.

Salvation is eternal, but this does not mean that Christians have no responsibility. What it *does* seem to support is that Christ Himself, through the Holy Spirit, *gifts* us with salvation, then yokes Himself with us throughout our earthly sojourn (cf. Matthew 11:30). We are not "in it" alone. Christ is there, promising to help us every step along the way (cf. John 6:37; 10:28; Hebrews 13:5; Jude 1:24-25).

Can Man Undo God's Seal?!
Paul also speaks of our being sealed with the Holy Spirit (cf. Ephesians 4:30). While he implores us *not* to grieve the Holy Spirit by willfully committing acts of sin, there is no indication that we are able somehow to break His seal. This sealing acts as a guarantee of what we *will* receive once we die. It is not an "if," "and," or "but" proposition. Paul refers specifically to this when he states, *"And when you heard the word of truth (the gospel of your salvation) – when you believed in Chris – you were marked with the seal of the promised Holy Spirit, who is the down payment of our inheritance, until the redemption of God's own possession, to the praise of his glory,"* (Ephesians 1:13 NET).

Paul also references this sealing in other places, such as 2 Corinthians 5:5, and 2 Corinthians 1:21. These and other passages of Scripture essentially refer to *ownership*. Paul states in 1 Corinthians 6:20 (NET), "*For you were bought at a price. Therefore glorify God with your body.*" He echoes this same truth in 1 Corinthians 7:23, NET, "*You were bought with a price. Do not become slaves of men.*"

If we have been purchased, so that we are no longer our own, how is it that we can somehow remove ourselves from the position of salvation? Certainly, from Paul's perspective, it would appear to be impossible. While it is feasible to go through Scripture and find statements that *seem* to indicate that a person must be baptized or something similar in order to receive salvation, the Bible, taken as a whole does not appear to support that belief. The fact remains then, that Warner and others who believe as he does, want to *add* something to salvation. Paul would have a few strong words for them because of their errant belief, which leads to works and arrogance.

However, though they err in their understanding of eternal security, they have the temerity to condemn the PreTrib Rapturist as someone who is not only deceived, but deceives others. For this, the payment is an eternity in hell, seen in this sentiment recently written to me in an email, "*There is a spirit of deception that has taken subtle control of Evangelicals and Fundamentalists in that regard. That is why I state that belief in a pretribulation rapture is a major contribution to the Great Apostasy.*"[48]

Sleeping in Spiritual Weakness?

This same individual – C. H. Fisher - stated to me in a separate correspondence, "*Consider the ramifications if you are wrong, and then consider the same if I am wrong. If you are wrong, many will sleeping in spiritual weakness, unprepared, apathetic, lethargic, and subject to apostasy, when the Antichrist gains control. If I am wrong I am simply*

---

[48] Email received from C. H. Fisher, dated 07/08/2009 at 6:07pm (on file)

*over-prepared for the PTR. I am not wrong because God's Word is not in error. **The problem is that you will continue believing a lie and assisting others in doing the same.** It is the sad truth and my heart breaks for the multitudes that are so deceived. However, my duty now and till the end is to prepare people who are willing to accept truth. I cannot do anything about those who refuse truth. **PTR, the Prosperity Doctrine, Unconditional Eternal Security, and other false doctrines will seal the doom of multitudes. Yet, they have shut their minds and will not hear.**"[49] (emphasis added)*

Mr. Fisher believes that he is correct, and that I, and other PreTrib Rapturists like myself, are 100% *incorrect*. That is not the problem. The problem comes into play when he lumps the PreTrib Rapture (PTR), and Unconditional Eternal Security together, labeling them as *false doctrines*, which "*will seal the doom of multitudes*." Therefore, the rather unfortunate part of believing a PreTrib Rapture position is the fallout from folks like Warner and Fisher, who seem to believe that this "deceptive" doctrine is one, which will send "multitudes" to hell.

It is incredibly easy for *all of us* to be so confident in our beliefs that we actually wind up closing off the possibility of any real dialogue. Certainly, it is important to *know* what the truth of Scripture states, but to act as if we wrote it, is another thing altogether.

Please note also, he believes that *if* he is wrong in his belief (that there is no Rapture prior to the Tribulation), he is simply "over-prepared". What can that possibly mean? Is Fisher somehow stating that he believes himself to be so spiritual, that if he is wrong about his Posttribulationalist position, his spirituality is such that he would stand unscathed by any temptation? Yet, if the PreTrib Rapturist happens to be the one who has believed and espoused an errant Eschatology, *his* mistake will likely lead him to *hell*? This is ludicrous,

---

[49] Email received from C. H. Fisher, dated 07/09/2009 at 7:49pm (on file)

yet Fisher obviously believes what he states, and does so with a straight face, as it were.

On the other hand, those who wait for the PreTrib Rapture are likely to be "*sleeping in spiritual weakness, unprepared, apathetic, lethargic, and subject to apostasy, when the Antichrist gains control.*" It is extremely difficult to see how the adoption of the PreTrib Rapture position, creates anything like the description Fisher presents.

The assumption on his part is that those who believe they will be taken off the planet prior to the terrible times of the coming Tribulation/Great Tribulation simply stop working. They stop praying. They stop studying their Bibles. They stop evangelizing. They essentially throw Christianity to the wind and say something along the lines of, "*Hey, I'm saved, and I'm getting out of here before the coming Tribulation, so I'm good to go! Now, to enjoy life!*" How utterly irrational is the person who holds that opinion of the PreTrib Rapturist?

With respect to the doctrine of Eternal Security, Fisher elaborates by stating, "*...it is another completely false doctrine that rode in on the same boat as PTR, and was disseminated by the same individual, C. I. Scofield, and his bible. [Unconditional eternal security, or UES] affords its adherents the premise (foundation) for committing all manner of sin under the blanket of a type of hell insurance policy.* **Like PTR proponents, UES proponents typically attack their opponents viciously, labeling them as heretics, evil people, hateful, judgmental, and etcetera, rather than simply accepting the Word of God.**"[50] (emphasis added)

One would think, from hearing Fisher tell it, that Scofield is to be blamed for the common cold. The truth of the matter is that eternal security goes back much further than C. I. Scofield, and while his implication is that the doctrine *did* go back prior to Scofield, he accuses

---

[50] Email received from C. H. Fisher, dated 07/09/2009 at 7:49pm (on file)

that it was not routinely accepted as fact *until* Scofield "disseminated it." In fact, it is odd that Fisher does not go back to the first century with respect to the arguments for and against eternal security. There are early church figures who were key in its development. However, going back to John Calvin would be sufficient for now. T.U.L.I.P. has as the "P," *perseverance of the saints*, which translates to *eternal security*. Scofield though, simply wrote about what appears in Scripture.

In fact, it is difficult to understand Fisher's *lack* of historical knowledge regarding this doctrine. It was essentially Calvin's thesis (1509-1564) vs. Arminius' (1560-1609) with respect to the doctrine of eternal security that put it in the limelight. Theologians have debated the two sides for centuries. Surely, Fisher cannot be so naïve to imply that prior to Scofield, the doctrine of eternal security, while known, was essentially *unheard* of, and that it was only through Scofield that the doctrine became widely recognized!

Because a person *might* misunderstand, and take advantage of God's grace, is *not* a good or logical argument against eternal security. What is also fascinating is how Fisher busily complains about the PreTrib Rapturist, as the one who uses caustic rejoinders and libelous terminology toward those who oppose them. From what has been quoted from Warner and a few others, though, it would appear that there is a good deal of muckraking from those opposed to the PreTrib Rapture position, as well as the doctrine of eternal security.

Spiritual Apathy Running Amok

Think of all the individuals who have written books on the PreTrib Rapture position, and the lives they have led, and do lead. While there are some that everyone enjoys pointing to, who are more noticeable for their antics, than their Christianity, most are people who love the Lord, long to be in His presence, honor Him with their lips as well as their hearts, and in general, strive to do the things that bring Him glory. They do not intentionally draw attention to themselves for the sake of ego, nor do they live outlandish, worldly lives.

I have not gotten the impression from any of these individuals that they have decided that since they will be saved from the coming Tribulation, they have no need to worry, nor do they really need to worry about living the Christian life. This is not only an absurd position for people like Warner and Fisher to hold, but it is one that is born of extreme conceit. They have literally placed themselves in a position of judging other Christians –the quality of their testimony and their standing before God – based *solely* on the fact that they have adopted a PreTrib Rapture position! Does this not seem absurd to anyone else, or is it just me?

Moreover, is not the position of Warner and Fisher, filled to the brim with a pride that is the result of seeing one's self *more* favorably than seeing others? It would certainly appear to be the case.

The visible Church is filled with plenty of *professing* Christians, but that should come as no surprise to authentic Christians, of which Christ warned us would exist, in the parable of the weeds, found in Matthew 13. In this section of Scripture, Jesus taught that counterfeit seed would be planted in the visible Church, which resembled the true seed. Nothing would be done about it until the "harvest."

> "*He presented them with another parable: 'The kingdom of heaven is like a person who sowed good seed in his field. But while everyone was sleeping, an enemy came and sowed weeds among the wheat and went away. When the plants sprouted and bore grain, then the weeds also appeared. So the slaves of the owner came and said to him, 'Sir, didn't you sow good seed in your field? Then where did the weeds come from?' He said, 'An enemy has done this.' So the slaves replied, 'Do you want us to go and gather them?' But he said, 'No, since in gathering the weeds you may uproot the wheat with them. Let both grow together until the harvest. At harvest time I will tell the reapers, "First collect the weeds and tie them in bundles to be burned, but then gather the wheat into my barn','*" (Matthew 13:124-30 NET).

Authentic vs. Professing Christians

The obvious problem is in recognizing whom the authentic Christians are, from those who are merely *professing* Christians. This is clearly not our job, though. If we look closely at the parable, notice the danger of uprooting the good *wheat,* along *with* the *tares,* or *weeds.* It was for this reason that the landowner told his workers to wait until the harvest. Fisher, on the other hand, gives the distinct impression that he *knows* who and who is not an authentic Christian by their "errant" belief in the PreTrib Rapture position. Then again, since Fisher does not believe in eternal security, it makes sense...*to him.* The truth of the matter though, is that if the "workers" (referring to angels), might make the mistake of "uprooting" the wrong plant, how much more might a human being? Whatever excuse he provides for himself, Fisher is merely looking on the *external,* believing that the outward provides an accurate picture of the inner man.

Fisher seems to be giving way too much weight to man's ability, and very little to God's sovereignty, along with His ability to keep those whom He has chosen.

Another problem with Fisher's reasoning has to do with the state of the visible Church. If we step back, and look carefully at the visible Church, we will see people who *profess* Christians, yet whose lives are anything *but* Christian, based on their actions, and words. This should be obvious, yet at the same time, we do *not* know how God might be working in their lives, to bring them to Him! We have no clue!

I would submit that there are many, *many* weak and even carnal Christians today, but to say that these somehow exist due to the Pre-Trib Rapture is a charge that is completely without merit. However, even a carnal Christian (if truly a Christian), will be saved, but everything else will burn up in the purifying fire of Jesus' judgment of believers. Paul is clear enough about this, in 1 Corinthians 3: *"If anyone builds on the foundation with gold, silver, precious stones, wood, hay, or straw, each builder's work will be plainly seen, for the Day will make it clear, because it will be revealed by fire. And the fire will test what kind of work each has done. If what someone has built survives, he will receive a reward. If someone's work is burned up, he will suffer loss. He himself will be saved, but only as through fire,"* (1 Corinthians 3:12-15).

In the quote above, Paul was writing to believers, who were carnal, immature and spiritual self-deceived. Thinking themselves to be something, they were actually nothing. They had not come to the point of understanding that salvation, while a spiritual transaction that cannot be undone, places responsibilities on the Christian. Those responsibilities include living a life that pleases the Lord. This is done only by submitting to His will in all things.

All Christians will one day stand before the Lord and our life will be replayed and judged, but not for salvation. It has everything to do with any rewards we might be given, in addition to the crown of life.

In this first letter to the Corinthians, Paul speaks out of frustration, because the believers there obviously did not understand the basics of Christianity, so he had to explain it to them...again. He was taking them to task for not only the way they lived, but also for the way they treated one another. This should not be and they needed to begin living correctly; doing those things which brought glory to the Lord. This was done only in the Lord's strength, not our own and that comes through submission to His will.

The point is simply, that it is *not* the *belief* (or a lack of belief), in the End Times, or even the belief in a PreTrib Rapture that makes a Christian spiritually strong, through maturity. What makes a Christian spiritually strong and mature is:

- *Spending time with God in His Word*
- *Spending time with God in prayer*

- *Seeking to live a life that honors Him*

The above bulleted list has to do with what should be the *normal*, daily life of the authentic Christian. Eschatological beliefs do not really enter the picture, except to bring to our minds the hope that we have in Christ. This hope should also translate into right living, which then becomes a testimony to the lost. Not only does John speak of this in 1 John 3:1-3, but Peter states,

> *"Blessed be the God and Father of our Lord Jesus Christ! By his great mercy he gave us new birth into a living hope through the resurrection of Jesus Christ from the dead, that is, into an inheritance imperishable, undefiled, and unfading. It is reserved in heaven for you, who by God's power are protected through faith for a salvation ready to be revealed in the last time.* **This brings you great joy**, *although you may have to suffer for a short time in various trials.* **Such trials show the proven character of your faith**, *which is much more valuable than gold – gold that is tested by fire, even though it is passing away – and will bring praise and glory and honor when Jesus Christ is revealed. You have not seen him, but you love him. You do not see him now but you believe in him, and so you rejoice with an indescribable and glorious joy, because you are attaining the goal of your faith – the salvation of your souls,"* (1 Peter 1:3-9 NET; emphasis added).

Note that among other things, Peter states that the thought of spending eternity with Christ *brings great joy*. Even though Peter warns the recipients of his letter *may have to suffer for a short time*. The joy of *expecting to see Christ*, either in the Rapture, at His Second Coming, or through death, *should* create within the Christian, tremendous joy.

Persecution *Proves <u>Existing</u>* Maturity – Does Not *Create* It!
Please notice also, that Peter points out the fact that trials do *not* create maturity in the believer. Trials are designed to *prove and re-*

fine the existing character of the believer. This is a huge difference, and one that is worthy of meditation and consideration. While we have people who complain about the PreTrib Rapture position, because *they* believe that it creates a compromising and apathetic spirit, Peter overrules them in this passage. He clearly states that trials and persecutions do *not* create, nor do they develop maturity in Christian character, but merely *prove* what is already within the Christian.

A Christian who is unprepared to face trials and persecutions is not due to a belief in the PreTrib Rapture. He is unprepared because he is immature in Christ, and likely just as ill-equipped to face the daily pressures of life, that trials and persecutions bring to the Christian, by virtue of the fact that the Christian stands in opposition to the Satanic worldview.

Christians need to face their own individual set of daily trials, in the strength of Christ. They need to be meeting them head on with prayer, supplication, humility, and a desire to do what Christ would have us do in each situation. Those who shrink from these daily pressures are going to do the exact same thing during the Tribulation/Great Tribulation, if the Rapture does not occur prior to it.

Those who mistakenly believe that the PreTrib Rapture will save them from the persecutions and trials of the Tribulation/Great Tribulation are probably already shrinking from life's trials. Moreover, those who preach that the PreTrib Rapture position is deadly, believing it to be born in hell, are preaching the wrong message. They erroneously believe that looking forward to escaping the coming wrath of God, is *wrong*. They believe that looking forward to escaping God's wrath that will be poured out over a seven year-period, is not only wrong, but terribly *wishful* thinking. This type of thinking – they assert – produces within the Christian the apathetic lifestyle that is seen in many Christians today. I fully reject this line of thinking, because it does not appear to be what it taught in Scripture.

Before moving on, let us sum up the problem that people see with the PreTrib Rapture position:

- *It engenders a false sense of security*
- *It creates apathy*
- *It manifests itself in spiritual immaturity*
- *It generates deception, because it is deceptive in and of itself*

These charges have not been proven, and *cannot* be proven, in spite of the amount of rhetoric that is bandied about, much of it filled with ridicule and anger. Those Christians, who are unable to face trials and persecutions *now*, will be no better able to face them *then*, during the Tribulation/Great Tribulation period, if the Rapture does precede it.

At the same time, for those Christians who are *watching* for the Lord, while *working* (completing His will for their life); they are concerned with doing things that please the Lord. It is often the *thought* or *consideration* of eternity itself that provides the impetus to live a life that glorifies Him. Deliberating on eternity, and one day being with Christ forever, does *not* promote laziness, spiritual apathy, or any other negative!

On the contrary, thinking about spending an eternity in the presence of Jesus Christ, our Savior, *promotes* right living! If we consider that He sees everything we do, hears everything we think, and notes everything that we say, what better motivation is there to do, say and live what is right, than realizing that He is near us? There is no better motivation at all.

It is no different from when I expected my father to return home after a day's work. As the time of his return approached, and I had not completed what he had assigned, my nervousness grew. I began to work feverishly, trying to complete the work he had given me before he arrived home. It was the thought of his return that provided the impetus. I should have had that thought all day long, though.

Considering Eternity is Legitimate

If I spend time thinking that the Lord is coming *soon* and might in fact, come *before* the Tribulation/Great Tribulation, how am I deceived because of it? There is *no* connection at all.

If a person can actually *think* of Jesus stepping out of the third heaven (like the father who opens the front door to the house), and calls His bride home to Him, someone needs to explain just *how* this promotes laziness. If this gives rise to laziness, the only reason would be because they are not thinking of Christ at all, but merely thinking of getting *out of here* before it really heats up!

Stopping to consider the fact of heaven, Jesus, the angels, and our loved ones who have gone on before us, neither *can,* nor should, *have any other* effect than to humbly bow before Him! There is absolutely no way to consider these things, then continue on with life, living in all type of sin, never reading the Word, or communicating with Him in prayer! It cannot be done and to blame a doctrine on the ineffectiveness of people who call themselves Christian is to beg the question, and to denigrate God's own ability to save those whom He has sealed through the Holy Spirit!

What about the Posttribulationists who say that Christians are to go through the Tribulation/Great Tribulation? Does anyone think for a moment that the Christians going through this upcoming period of time (if the Posttribulationist is correct), will *not* be thinking *of,* and praying *to,* Jesus almost without ceasing? Is it difficult to think that these individuals will *not* be spending all of their time wishing for, waiting for, and looking forward to, eternity with Christ, hoping for His soon return.

The Posttribulationist apparently believes that persecution *prompts* authentic Christian growth within the Christian. Yet, we have seen from at least one apostle (Peter), that trials and persecutions *prove* what is already within each individual. If a Christian is not mature, because he spends no time in Bible study, in prayer, or in fellowship with other believers, then that existing character will also be *proven* in situations, which bring trials and persecutions. For that Christian, what will be seen during those times is what exists within him *now*; namely, an inability to handle those situations.

Lack of Bible Study, Prayer and Fellowship = Failure!

The idea that persecution makes a Christian mature is a *fallacy*; a fallacy that is born of a severe lack of knowledge regarding God's Word and the way He works in and through His children.

God does not put the cart before the horse, by stating that He is going to send us persecution and trials and through those things, we will learn what it is like to become mature Christians! While persecution will likely *drive* an authentic Christian to their knees, it is also very likely to cause an immature (or especially a *professing*), Christian to do exactly what all of the apostles did (including Peter), the night Jesus was arrested. They all *fled*, and in Peter's case, while he hung around to see what was happening, he wound up *denying* the fact that he even *knew* Jesus!

The terrible truth of the matter is that those who believe and teach that the PreTrib Rapture is wrong because they believe it creates weak, immature and deceived Christians, seem not to understand the Bible, the way the Holy Spirit teaches, and how it is that Christians become mature in the first place. It certainly appears as though Peter would disagree with their assumptions, as well as John.

Emerging Darkness

The fact that many Christians today are weak, immature, and bereft of spiritual strength, has everything to do with the state of the visible

Church today. The state of the visible Church has *nothing* to do with a wrong or right view of Eschatology, and everything to do with the fact that the Emerging Church has gained such a strong foothold within Christendom.

Do Posttribulationalists like Dave MacPherson and others honestly believe that the Emerging Church has had *no negative* impact on Christians today? It would seem so, due to their proclivity to reserve their condemnation mainly for the PreTrib Rapture position, and those who believe and espouse it.

The Emergent Church has done much to water down Christianity, even *recreating* Jesus into something He is not. Proponents of, and leaders within, the Emergent Movement, have all but removed the deity from Christ. Salvation, for those leaders within the Emergent Church, has become so muddled that it no longer has the same Scriptural boundaries it enjoyed when the Church first began.

Tony Campolo on Salvation

Tony Campolo is a leading proponent in the Emergent Church, with its emphasis on a social gospel. He espouses it continually, and without apology.

In an Interview with Tony Campolo by Shane Claiborne, Campolo defines salvation in a number of ways, as seen in the following quotations:

> *"I've got to believe that Jesus is the only Savior but being a Christian is not the only way to be saved."*

> *"When it comes to what is ultimately important, the Muslim community's sense of commitment to the poor is exactly in tune with where Jesus is in the 25th chapter of Matthew. That is the description of judgment day. And if that is the description of judgment day what can I say to an Islamic brother who has fed the hungry, and clothed the naked? You say, 'But he hasn't a per-*

sonal relationship with Christ.' I would argue with that. And I would say from a Christian perspective, in as much as you did it to the least of these you did it unto Christ. **You did have a personal relationship with Christ, you just didn't know it.** *And Jesus himself says: 'On that day there will be many people who will say, when did we have this wonderful relationship with you, we don't even know who you are. . . ' 'Well, you didn't know it was me, but when you did it to the least of these it was doing it to me'."* (emphasis added)

"Our Muslim brothers and sisters can say Islam is the only true faith but we are not convinced that only Muslims enjoy salvation. I contend that there is no salvation apart from Jesus Christ, but I am not convinced that the grace of God does not go further than the Christian community."

"We end up with this mishmash in which we say, 'Well, in the end, we all believe in the same God'. Maybe we do, but we don't define God in the same way. We don't come to God in the same manner. And each of us makes exclusivist claims, and we have to recognize that. We cannot allow our theologies to separate us, and we cannot allow our theologies to get watered down lest we lose our integrity."

"I think that what we all have to do is leave judgment up to God. The Muslim community is very evangelistic, however what Muslims will not do is condemn Jews and Christians to Hell if in fact they do not accept Islam."

"Rather than making theological statements, we need to tell each other our stories. Jesus would tell stories and then say, 'what do you make of this story?'..."

All of the above quotes were taken from the same interview,[51] and what we gain from the entire interview, along with the pulled quotes, is that Campolo has a difficulty drawing the line between what is correct theology and what is incorrect theology. There is plenty of this type of thinking going on within the Emergent Church. Because of this thinking, it has attracted multitudes of *professing* Christians, which have swelled the ranks.

PreTrib Rapture vs. Emergent Church

Yet, Posttribulationalists like Dave MacPherson, seemingly ignore the Emergent Church, firmly believing that it is the *PreTrib Rapture* position, which *is* deceptive, and *creates* more deception, to the point that people will be driven to hell because of it. Why do we not hear these same individuals decrying the problems within the Emergent Church? A trip to Tim Warner's site finds no mention of the deception espoused by the Emergent Church.[52] All of the articles and sermons posted, deal only with Eschatology, most in the form of rebuttals to the PreTrib Rapture position.

However, what is worse is the claim that a few people were able to develop a hoax, which in turn, became large enough to deceive many to most individuals within modern evangelicalism. We will look at that in our next chapter.

---

[51] http://www.crosscurrents.org/CompoloSpring2005.htm
[52] http://answersinrevelation.org/

Chapter 6
A Fisherman's Tale

There exists today, within a growing segment of Christendom, a generally-accepted and burgeoning belief that began with Margaret MacDonald, and went from her to Edward Irving, and from him to J. N. Darby, and finally, to C. I. Scofield. This belief is enumerated as a well-crafted hoax, born of Darby, and carried on by Scofield, which has been ultimately foisted upon evangelicalism, since the late 1800s. The belief further states that if not for Scofield, what Darby had created (Darbyism or the roots of Dispensationalism), which is, among other things, the idea of the PreTrib Rapture, would never have lasted.

It is difficult to know exactly where to start, to either confirm or negate this claim. Certainly, church history will shed some light on this, but other sources may be needed as well. The reality though, is that so many have entered the fray, it has become increasingly difficult to know which historical fact is actually fact. No doubt, in this case, it is much better to deal with Scripture, and let the chips fall where they may. However, an overview of observations from those who believe the alleged hoax will also shed light on the subject.

Fishing, Hook, Line and Sinker

In his ebook, *Pretribulation Rapture: What If It Isn't True?*, C. H. Fisher does not shy away from presenting his own ideas concerning the hows and whys of Darbyism, and how it took hold. In chapter five, he details, the scenario that *he* believes took place, which allowed what has come to be known as Darbyism (by its detractors), to reach untold heights of acceptance, because of one man; C. I. Scofield.

Fisher states, "*How did so many people come to accept Dispensationalism and the secret pretribulation rapture theory of John Nelson Darby? There is no doubt that Darbyism would have fallen into obscurity and never been heard of again if it had not been for C. I. Scofield and his reference bible. Scofield's reference bible broke the time-honored tradition that all the Bible societies had conformed to of printing Bibles without the opinions of men included. In fact, as someone has suggested, if Scofield had written his notes as a companion book to the Bible, his book would have been destined to the same fate, as many such books eventually met. However, the world was ripe for Scofield's Bible, especially in the rapidly progressing American society. From the beginning, America was destined to become multi-cultured nation of common people, most of them uneducated, who spilled out of Europe, Africa, and various other parts of the world into a land of hope and promise. Many who populated this vast continent were fleeing the heavy hand of social, economic, and religious oppression. However, some were forced to come to America because of other reasons. They brought only what they deemed necessary to survive the harsh climate of the new nation. Many also brought their belief systems, which even-*

tually became meshed together as the old generations died and their offspring married people of other beliefs."[53]

It is An Obscure Matter...

Fisher states without equivocation (*or* documentation), that Darbyism would have fallen into "obscurity" without the help of Scofield. Fisher then proceeds to give us a history lesson, involving the burgeoning growth of the telegraph system, which by the late 1800s, had been replaced by electricity and telephones. Because of this technological growth in our nation's history, information became more readily available. This in turn, according to Fisher, was an apparent boon for Scofield, and had a cathartic effect for the average American evangelical.

Fisher claims that Scofield's study system Bible upped the ante. He states, *"Bursting on the scene of this budding age of industry was the spurious Scofield Reference Bible. For the person who did not have time to read and study the history of Christianity, who did not have time to study the Bible for himself or herself, and who did not read well enough to gather or grasp the meaning of the Scriptures, Scofield was ready to feed and divert him from historical theology. Scofield gave the people the quick and easy way to study the Bible so that they had more time to engage in the endless activities of a burgeoning nation. What the church leaders failed to grasp in allowing the Scofield Bible to reach fame and acceptance was that a trend would develop that would eventually prove to be the downfall of millions. The paradigm would shift from honor of the Word of God to a cavalier mishandling of the Scriptures until they would no longer be given the reverence and awe of ages past. The printed Word of God would fall into the hands of unscrupulous men who would add their own words to the pages, stamp their own names onto the cover, and by degrees, turn the Bible into a book of scripture mingled with fatuous opinions. The historic compass of the Scriptures had always been used to point faithfully at the true*

---

[53] http://www.truthkeepers.com/chapter_five.htm

path; now that path became shrouded in a maze of new directions. The old landmarks would be grown over with the suffocating weeds of human error, causing multitudes to lose the way to truth and an intimate relationship with God."[54]

Smells Like Opinion to Me!

Aside from his opinionated rhetoric, it is clear that Fisher believes that what Darby 'made up,' based on the questionable vision of a 15 year-old girl, Scofield incorporated into his own system of study, ultimately publishing it as a Bible with notes. From these notes, Scofield managed to turn the evangelical world on its head, removing the visible Church from its previously moored (and no doubt, Fisher believes, *sanctified*) location, leading it off into the darkness of deception and error. These are libelous charges Fisher and others bring against Darby and Scofield. It is a shame that neither man is here to offer a rebuttal and defense against them.

Could it be anymore clear from Fisher's book, that he has no love or respect for Scofield, or Darby? To him, they are deceivers, and deceivers deserve the darkest place in hell. Just prior to getting into his critique of Scofield's study system Bible itself, he introduces that section with these comments, *"This modern church craves the quick fix of sound bite religion sprinkled with sensationalism.* ***Pretribulation Rapture, Unconditional Eternal Security, and the materialistic Prosperity doctrine*** *have found a fertile field in this current age. Did Scofield cause all of this to come about? Is his reference Bible responsible for the dawning of apostasy on this mighty nation? I would say that he has to share a great portion of the blame, because he opened the door for the plague of* ***Scripture tampering*** *and he was a primary promoter of false doctrine in the first half of the twentieth century."*[55] (emphasis added)

---

[54] http://www.truthkeepers.com/chapter_five.htm
[55] http://www.truthkeepers.com/chapter_five.htm

What is this "Scripture tampering," of which Fisher refers? Is Fisher upset because Scofield provided his opinion about what the Bible *states*? Did C. I. Scofield *actually* and *tenaciously* revise, or tamper with the Word of God?

What?! You Mean It's Not in the Church History Books?!

Fisher certainly holds nothing back when it comes to Scofield. What is most interesting though is that none of the following books dealing with Church History even *mentions* Darby, or Scofield. Of the five listed, only *Christianity Through the Centuries*, barely mentions *Dispensationalism*, dedicating a mere two pages to the subject.

- *Church History in Plain English Language*, by Bruce Shelley
- *Christianity Through the Centuries*, by Earle E. Cairns
- *Charts of Christian Theology and Doctrine*, by H. Wayne House
- *Kregel Pictorial Guide to Church History*, by John D. Hannah
- *Introduction to the History of Christianity*, Tim Dowley, Ed.

Fisher himself quotes from Bruce Shelley's book on church history, and yet, if the environment and the situation surrounding Darby and then Scofield, was such that a vast movement was created, why is it not even *mentioned* in any of the books above? Surely, at least a few books would touch on the subject, of Darby, Scofield, or Dispensationalism.

In the book, *Chronological and Background Charts of Church History*, by Robert C. Walton, both Darby and Scofield are listed by name (only), on page 95 and again on page 111. There is neither commentary about them, nor information regarding any movement that they may have begun.

Certainly, someone will argue that the hoax or deception, extended to those who have written, and do write about church history as well. However, it seems obvious enough that the situation concerning both Darby and Scofield did *not* create a large enough condition in America (or anywhere else, for that matter), to warrant any real notice. In spite of this, people like Fisher, Warner and MacPherson, et al, would have us believe their accusations, regardless of whether or not they stretch the boundaries of believability.

History After Darby and Scofield

One can only wonder why Scofield's Bible took off as well as it did. Fisher has his own ideas, which he does not hesitate to share; "*The people of God became merchandised by the Scofield Reference Bible. By inference, they have all become stupid, incapable of interpreting the Bible for themselves on an issue that pretribulationist's (sic) declare is 'plainly there in the Scripture's for all to see.' I have noticed that some pretribulationist's (sic) have offered 'rapture kits' for sale with advertisements that declare that the kit contains 'everything you need to understand this complicated doctrine called the Rapture.' There are even things to leave for your loved ones and acquaintances that are left behind'.*"[56]

It is impossible to know which "pretribulationists" have offered rapture kits for sale, since Fisher offers absolutely *no* documentation at all, to support his statements. Having done our own search on the Internet, we came up with the following:

- *http://www.raptureanswers.com/letter.htm* - This site boasts a personal letter from someone named Bekah. In it, she explains what happened to her, and explains not only the Rapture, but also the gospel. We were unable to locate anything on her site that was for sale.
- *http://www.rapture-survival-kit.com/the_rapture_survival_kit* - another site which explains what happens during the Rapture. Quite a few links and recommendations, along with pictures, which show the items they have included in their own Rapture kit, as well as instructions and resources to include if the reader

---

[56] http://www.truthkeepers.com/chapter_five.htm

would like to make their own. Noted nothing for sale on this site either.

- *http://rapturesurvival.blogspot.com/* - a site where the Rapture is discussed. Nothing for sale there.
- *http://www.doomsdayguide.org/Video/page_017.htm* - offers a video of what the meaning of the Rapture. Still nothing for sale.
- *http://englishatheist.org/indexn.shtml* - This one is a *pre*-Rapture kit. Nothing for sale here, either. Simply an atheist who has plans for the stuff Christians leave behind when the Rapture occurs.

Again, it would have been nice if Fisher had backed up his claims with some actual documentation, but he failed to include any such references. Since we were unable to locate any on the web, we have to conclude that either he is making it up, or all of the sites that he said existed, have been taken down, since he wrote his book.

"Dangerously Close!"

Fisher plods onward, claiming *"Many prominent pretribulationists are coming dangerously close to declaring that anyone who does not believe in PTR will be left behind, no matter how godly that they may be. In fact, I have heard this concept insinuated from the pulpit several times, always with the tone of scorn and ridicule toward those who do not believe in PTR. The masses are taught to believe that it is a disqualification for Heaven to disbelieve PTR. This is backed up with the fact that those who dare disbelieve it are dismissed from fellowship in some denominations. As a result, the people fear to let truth come in about the matter. But do pretribulation rapturists really know the truth?"*[57]

Again, Mr. Fisher provides no documentation whatsoever, apparently expecting us to take his word for it. The problem though, is that it would be ridiculous for anyone to take his word for it, just as it would be ridiculous for anyone to take *my* word for what is printed within

---

[57] http://www.truthkeepers.com/chapter_five.htm

these pages, if I made declarative statements without providing factually documented proof of such claims.

Frankly, this author is unaware of any fellowship, or church that insinuates from the pulpit or otherwise, that those who do not accept the PreTrib Rapture position, will be dismissed from that fellowship. While it is possible they exist, their existence makes no sense, if they have policies predicated on the acceptance of the PreTrib Rapture. In fact, the church that this author attends, and is a member of (an IFCA Church), includes people who accept aspects of Covenant Theology, and do *not* accept the Rapture – PreTrib or otherwise. Their decision to remain with the church is theirs, and they are welcome.

Just as importantly, *if* the PreTrib Rapture position is the correct position (for the sake of argument), there is nothing that can be pointed to in Scripture indicating a Posttribulationalist would *not* be taken in the Rapture, and would remain on earth. Everyone who is an *authentic Christian* at the time of the Rapture goes...whether they like it or not (or believe it or not). How could it be otherwise, especially if we consider the fact that the invisible Church is *the* Bride of Christ? Why – for goodness sake – would Jesus leave part of His Bride here, just because they did not believe and espouse a PreTrib Rapture position? He would not, and the charge that He would is ridiculous.

A Good Deal in Common
There is still a great deal of commonality between believers who do not agree in matters of Eschatology. While Fisher seems to display his own scorn for these alleged churches that excommunicate people for their views on Eschatology, he appears to be doing the very same thing with many of the statements he has made regarding the PreTrib Rapture position, and those who believe it. Does the reader need to be reminded of Fisher's words said to this author regarding the deception of the PreTrib Rapture position?

*"PTR, the Prosperity Doctrine, Unconditional Eternal Security,
and other false doctrines will seal the doom of multitudes. Yet,
they have shut their minds and will not hear."[58]*

Therefore, while Fisher complains that people are (allegedly) coming "dangerously close" to saying those who do not believe the PreTrib Rapture will be left behind, he is actually saying something much worse! He is stating that the "doom" of these folks will be sealed. What can Fisher possibly mean by that statement except that they are "dangerously close" to going to hell, and many *will* end up there?

*"Because of belief in this deadly doctrine, UES [Unconditional Eternal Security] proponents have no compunction to consider PTR [Pretrib Rapture] might be false. After all, **if they are wrong and cause millions to enter everlasting damnation**, God will still say to them, 'Well done, My good and faithful servant, enter into the joys of the Lord.' What a tragic deception. No wonder that individuals who believe one of these heresies also believe the other one."[59]* (emphasis added)

The above are Fisher's own words in an email. He believes people who espouse the PreTrib Rapture doctrine, are on a one-way path. This path leads directly to hell (everlasting damnation). None of the reasons Fisher has stated for *why* people might go to hell, if they believe and espouse the PreTrib Rapture doctrine, have any merit biblical whatsoever.

The Immature and Unspiritual Christian

The worst-case scenario is that if the PreTrib Rapture position is *incorrect*, then many who believe it, and are alive when the Tribulation occurs, will go *through* it. It is as simple as that. Those who believed it as *easy escapism*, in truth, are probably *not* authentic Christians in the final analysis. They certainly have no depth about them, in the

---

[58] Email received from C. H. Fisher, dated 07/09/2009 at 7:49pm (on file)
[59] Email received from C. H. Fisher, dated 07/13/2009 at 9:42pm (on file)

first place. When they came across the PreTrib Rapture position, they grabbed hold of it (intellectually), for all the *wrong* reasons.

The PreTrib Rapture position did *not* define their spiritual character, or lack of maturity and growth. They were there already, and misunderstood the tenure of the PreTrib Rapture at the start. These are the types of Christians who do not like *any* form of trial, or persecution. They routinely run from it. Worse, they constantly verbally attack and question God *because of it.*

"Why, God?! Why did you allow this?!" they wail and moan. His response (not that He has to give one), is, "*I AM that I AM. I am sovereign, and I do what I do because it is right and I can do nothing else!*" Is it any reason Paul, in Romans, stated essentially, "*who do you think you are, questioning God! Does the thing that is being made, speak back to the one making it?!*" (cf. Romans 9:19-21)

It would appear that those who disallow the PreTrib Rapture position are often on the *giving* end of the scorn and ridicule, as has been evidenced by the many quotes from some of these individuals throughout this book. It appears as though Fisher is making a mountain out of a molehill. While it is obvious that Scofield had an impact on American society, the idea that he *intentionally* created a mass cover-up for the purposes of selling his Bible is strained to say the least. Fisher should be ashamed of himself.

But what of any *positive* effects that came from Darby and Scofield? Certainly, folks like Fisher and Warner would say that *none* came forth, however, it is clear that more people started reading their Bibles. That alone is a positive that cannot be ignored. If more people were reading their Bibles, then more people were also likely attending church and entering into Bible studies and discussions about the End Times and other doctrinal areas. MacPherson, Fisher, Warner et al, certainly downplay these positives into non-existence.

But maybe there were other events and circumstances which were occuring in the world, and more specifically in America, which provided just the right type of environment to allow Scofield's views to the come to the fore. After all, the entrance of PreTrib Rapturism came into being, in *spite* of the fact that Posttribulationism was supposedly a major factor in religious belief and instruction at the time. So, what, if anything, could have shined so favorably on Scofield's views that they were literally catapulted to the top of the heap, effectively burying Posttribulationalism?

A Bit of Actual History
As often happens in any society, the pendulum swings from one extreme to the other. Life seems "best" when it is somewhere in the middle, however, it does not seem to stay there for long. There are many factors which make the pendulum swing, and there are many factors, which keep it moving from one side to the other.

For Fisher and others, it appears as though Darby and Scofield bear the brunt of the responsibility in creating and dispensing an alleged man-made doctrine called the PreTrib Rapture. As in anything though, it is not merely the relating of facts of history (questionable, or otherwise), that unveil the truth, but it is the *context* in which those facts (questionable, or otherwise), actually *occurred*.

History reveals a great deal. Pick up a copy of *The Timetables of History,* by Bernard Grun, published by Touchestone/Simon & Schuster (ISBN 9780671742713). It is over 720 pages of extremely useful, historical information.

A number of years prior to Scofield's birth, people like Joseph Smith, Charles Darwin, Helena Petrova Blavatsky, Karl Marx, Dwight D. Moody, Ira Sankey, and Charles Taze Russell had already been born. These people had already had some effect on America and the world, by the time Scofield introduced the Scofield Study System Bible.

There had been plenty of wars, secessions, abdications, one country taking over another, and then losing newly won territory back. Assasinations of President Lincoln and others had already taken place. Mary Baker Eddy was born the year after the Scofield Study System Bible was introduced to the public.

As the years from 1909 progressed, World War I began, which made the world officially, much more connected. This is the *actual* first world war, unlike Richard Abanes' claim that the real first war was the War of Spanish Succession (as he posits in his book *End- Times Visions*). This stems from the beliefs of two, deceased historians. At any rate, what now happened overseas, was heard about much more quickly in America.

There were also a few minor to major depressions in America, however nothing like the coming Stock Market Crash of 1929. We are also likely aware of how the Roaring Twenties came in on a literal roar, and went out with a good deal of gunfire.

Truth be told, the times in the world were very difficult at best. It is most definitely *not* clear that Posttribulationalists were getting their message across and if so, it would appear that folks were not generally interested in it. Doctrines from Replacement Theologians, or those from the Roman Catholic Church had for a long time, allegorized Scripture, based on Augustine's interpretations of it. Since Augustine successfully created a way for Christianity to divorce itself from Judaism, the result was that the Church was *now* the new Israel. All promises made to Israel in the Old Testament, would now be fulfilled in the Church.

"Augustine admitted that at one time he had espoused the prominent doctrine of 'Chiliasm' the sound biblical truth that was taught by the apostles, the belief in a future millennium, in which the Church and redeemed Israel will be blessed by the personal return and reign of Christ on the earth. However, he had since come to what he calls 'more

satisfactory' view that the Church has replaced Israel forever. Jerusalem and the Temple were destroyed in fulfillment of prophecy, and the Jews were dispersed throughout the Roman Empire. The question would be, which of Augustine views is more sound; the previous views he espoused, or his newer one? In other words, which doctrine is more sound, the original one, or the one that has been used longer? One would think that the original supersedes, it is closer to what the apostles taught and to what their master Jesus Christ taught as well."[60]

Moving Forward

In the 1920s onward, it was this type of theological rhetoric that was being routinely taught and accepted throughout the world and certainly, within Roman Catholic Churches of America. Unfortunately, "'Christendom' canonized Augustine's evil ideas by establishing him as an official saint, and theologians throughout the Roman Empire accepted his false doctrine."[61]

What is sadly intriguing is that, like today's PreTrib Rapturist, "The Chiliasts were branded as holding 'aberrant and heretical views', and Augustinian Replacement Theology with other false theologies became the 'cornerstone' of the Roman Catholic concepts. In the later developments in the Eastern Orthodox Church, the European Reformation and the Anglican split, Replacement Theology continued essentially untouched. It was an important part of the standard Christian view of Israel, the world, and prophecy. This view which 'evolved' had no basis in what the Apostles taught, on the contrary, instead of being Biblical became anti-Biblical as cursing Israel in reality is cursing God's chosen people since Roman persecution, the Holocaust, and the Russian Pogroms and the inquisitions used this type

---

[60] http://www.cephas-library.com/replacement_theology/replacement_theology_history.html
[61] Ibid

of theology in order to destroy the Jew. How can anyone claim Biblical Christianity and support this view and not seeing the dangers?"[62]

Even though Posttribulationalists state that *their* view was the majority view held during the time of Scofield, it must be acknowledged that it was *not* the only view espoused. Replacement Theology in some form, which had been around since Augustine, replaced Chiliasm, yet on the basis of the fact that Augustine dates to the second/third centuries, many believe it should not be questioned. However, *everything* should be questioned and compared with Scripture, regardless of its age. The idea that because something is *old*, or has been accepted for centuries, makes it more viable is simply incorrect, as Augustinian Eschatology shows.

Age Does Not Make It Correct

"'Replacement Theology's misguided approach to the Bible not only led millions of Christians astray over the years but it has, in addition, birthed evil of the most horrific proportions. Replacement Theology played a role in the persecution of Jews by the church through the centuries, including the Holocaust.' (quote by Malcolm Hedding), since all the promises and blessings and Israel's entire inheritance, now belongs to the Church while Israel gets to keep the curses."[63]

The above is routinely *denied* today by Replacement Theologians, and would also have to be denied by those who see the PreTrib Rapture position as part of the End Times deception. Yet, there it is, with the results fully in view.

One has to wonder why those opposed to PreTrib Rapturists, have their harshest words for *them*, virtually ignoring the fallacies of Replacement Theology and its history? This limited eyesite that many possess, does nothing except create an artificial situation

---

[62] http://www.cephas-library.com/replacement_theology/replacement_theology_history.html
[63] Ibid

where the PreTrib Rapture is concerned. It blindly ignores the prejudices and hatred espoused by those who believe and advocate a Replacement Theology position.

What If It Makes Sense?

The fact is that people *could have* adopted Scofield's understanding of the End Times, due simply to the fact that it makes *sense!* With the American society facing the rigors of the Great Depression, various tumultuous wars occuring throughout the world, having to deal with the ravages of Communism, Socialism, and Darwinism, which gained steam, it certainly appeared as though Replacement Theology had a reason to exist. This, and other viewpoints like it, expressed a belief that the world would simply get *better* as Christians did more work evangelizing the lost, and by doing so, would effect a greater positive change within society, which would allow Jesus to return. Yet, has this actually been the result of such action? Do we see less war, terrorism, hatred and the like today? No, we do not. If anything, we are experiencing *more* of these things across the globe.

The betterment of society and the world has not been happening, in spite of what we are led to believe, by these same type of proponents, who are now part of the Emergent Church system. Embracing what Darby systematized, and Scofield published, might very well have been an answer people were looking for, during a time in which everything seemed bleak. Certainly, the ideologies of Replacement Theology have done *nothing* to improve society.

The people of the Great Depression, knew what it was like to go without, and to suffer. They were also some of the hardest working people this country has ever had the privilege of having live here.

What Darby and Scofield espoused, was *infinitely* greater than a PreTrib Rapture. What they espoused, *began* to change the course of the visible Church, with respect to the anti-Semitism that had long prevailed. Instead of seeing the nation of Israel as something God no longer wanted to deal with, the Church was now being forced to rethink its position on major covenants of the Old Testament!

The Church was asking questions such as, "*Has the Church replaced Israel? If so, what does that mean for the Church? If not, what does that mean for Israel?*"

They wondered about Romans 9-11, when Paul stated explicitly that a Jew is not one who is one outwardly, but one who is one inwardly. "*What does that mean? Does Paul mean that as a Gentile believer, I am now a spiritual Jew?!*" Not if context means anything at all. In that entire passage, Paul is referring *only* to Jews, and he was comparing and contrasting an *outward* Jew, with a Jew who was a Jew *inwardly*, *by faith* in God. He was *not* talking about, or to Gentiles in that section of Scripture. He was talking to, and about Jews only.

What did Paul mean when he spoke of the fact that all Israel would be saved? A Replacement Theologian teaches that it means that through the Church (the new Israel), Israel would be saved. But that seemed to beg the question, because throughout Romans, Paul keeps Gentiles and Jews virtually *separate*, never combining them into one.

Even in his letter to the Galatians, when speaking of the two shall become one man, he is speaking of the *spiritual* realm, not this *present* world. If that is the case, then it must be extended to slaves and free, and men and woman as well. Yet, Paul showed no inclination to teach that all slaves should be set free. However, he understood that *in Christ*, they were truly free *already*.

Scofield, and his Study System Bible, was a *response* to the erroneous viewpoints of the Church, which existed at the time. Is the Scofield Study System Bible perfect? No, but nothing is perfect in our age. As far as we know, we do not possess a set of original autographs of the Bible, signed by Moses, or by God. We trust, however, that what we *do* have is something that still enables us to ascertain what God wants us to know about Him and His will. This occurs through the revelation of His truth through the Holy Spirit.

The times which existed during the lives of Darby and later Scofield, were such that the error that had become commonly accepted as truth, and desperately needed to be dispelled. Scofield's Study System Bible gave people reason to do that. Far from creating a heretical system of deception, it caused godly men and women to begin to question anew their commitment to God, His Word, and His as-yet, unfulfilled plans and purposes for Israel.

Chapter 7
An Acrimonious Assault

With the amount of acrimony directed toward the PreTrib Rapturist, through charges, implications, and inferences, it is evident that this belief is viewed as something that is directly born of deceit, and passed on as such. From as often as he uses it, one of Dave MacPherson's favorite words used to describe PreTrib Rapturists appears to be "promoters."

MacPherson makes a grand production out of attempting to prove that Grant Jeffrey's opinions are not only in error, but have completely covered things over with the Pseudo-Ephraim document, so that it says something other than what it actually states. This document is believed to be from the 3rd to the 5th century, or earlier and describes the time during the end of the age. It is a bit ambiguous in parts, or at least not fully clear, which has led people from all corners of Eschatology to believe that it supports *their* position. No one is clear on the authorship and the use of the "pseudo" in the title points to this.

MacPherson boasts in an article, *"Nevertheless, Grant Jeffrey in his 1995 book, FINAL WARNING, had the audacity to claim that P-E "began with the Rapture using the word 'imminent' and added in the next sentence that Ephraem used the word 'imminent' to describe the Rapture." **(If he and other P-E promoters can look at a coming of Antichrist and see a coming of "Christ,"** is it any wonder that in his end-time view folks will look at Antichrist and see "Christ"? Ephraim the Syrian, reportedly P-E's inspiration, said the same thing (SERMO AS-CETICUS, I): "Nothing remains then, except that the coming of our enemy, Antichrist, appear...." (Nobody's ever found even a trace of pre-trib in this earlier work!)."*[64] (emphasis added)

In fact, MacPherson's last sentence in parentheses has no bearing on anything. Whether or not any "PreTrib" reference can be seen in an earlier work, does not make or break the Pseudo-Ephraem document's validity, nor does it affect the document writer's integrity. Theology, especially in those early days, underwent a *process* of development. To assume that there had to have been a reference to a PreTrib rapture in an *earlier* work, is to assume that his theology never changed and/or *developed*. However, even MacPherson has agreed that the authorship of the Pseudo-Ephraem document remains in question (*"Pseudo-Ephraem - hereafter: P-E - , the name attached by scholars to manuscripts that were possibly, but not provably, written by the well-known Ephraim the Syrian who lived from 306-373 A.D."*). Just because some assume it to be from Ephraim, the Syrian, does not mean that it *is* his work, as MacPherson seems to agree to, in which case, any omission of the PreTrib Rapture would be normal.

---

[64] http://www.thewordsofeternallife.com/deceived.html

Let us look at the document in question and then the reader can decide what the document states. MacPherson points to Section 2 of the 10-section document, because that is what Jeffrey is quoting. Here is the section in its entirety:

> "*We ought to understand thoroughly therefore, my brothers, what is imminent or overhanging. Already there have been hunger and plagues, violent movements of nations and signs, which have been predicted by the Lord, they have already been fulfilled (consummated), and there is not other which remains, except the advent of the wicked one in the completion of the Roman kingdom. Why therefore are we occupied with worldly business, and why is our mind held fixed on the lusts of the world or on the anxieties of the ages? Why therefore do we not reject every care of worldly business, and why is our mind held fixed on the lusts of the world or on the anxieties of the ages? Why therefore do we not reject every care of earthly actions and prepare ourselves for the meeting of the Lord Christ, so that he may draw us from the confusion, which overwhelms all the world? Believe you me, dearest brother, because the coming (advent) of the Lord is nigh, believe you me, because the end of the world is at hand, believe me, because it is the very last time. Or do you not believe unless you see with your eyes? See to it that this sentence be not fulfilled among you of the prophet who declares: "Woe to those who desire to see the day of the Lord!" **For all the saints and elect of God are gathered, prior to the tribulation that is to come, and are taken to the Lord lest they see the confusion that is to overwhelm the world because of our sins.** And so, brothers most dear to me, it is the eleventh hour, and the end of the world comes to the harvest, and angels, armed and prepared, hold sickles in their hands, awaiting the empire of the Lord. And we think that the earth exists with blind infidelity, arriving at its downfall early. Commotions are brought forth, wars of diverse peoples and battles and incursions of the barbarians threaten,*

and our regions shall be desolated, and we neither become very much afraid of the report nor of the appearance, in order that we may at least do penance; because they hurl fear at us, and we do not wish to be changed, although we at least stand in need of penance for our actions!"[65] (emphasis added)

The first sentence is essentially, what MacPherson is referring to here. The writer of the document is referencing something that is imminent. He refers to *hunger and plagues, wars and rumoring of wars,* etc. He speaks of the coming wicked one, which is an obvious reference to the Antichrist. This is what MacPherson is poking fun at, regarding Jeffrey, believing that Jeffrey was saying that the use of the word imminent meant the Rapture was going to occur, but MacPherson is stating that the writer of the document seemed to be referring to the Antichrist, or 'wicked one'. It appears as though MacPherson is using *deceptive* means to imply that Jeffrey is confused regarding the difference between Jesus and the Antichrist.

However, please note that MacPherson, though ridiculing Jeffrey, pays no attention to the section that we have bolded. In it, the writer of the document *clearly* states that "**all the saints and elect of God are gathered, prior to the tribulation that is to come, and are taken to the Lord.**" Now, what does this mean, except that the writer of the document intended it to mean that *all the saints and elect...are taken prior to the tribulation?* The very words are *in* the document itself!

MacPherson comments on this statement from the Pseudo-Ephraem document, by deferring to Dr. Paul Alexander. MacPherson states,

"Dr. Paul Alexander, the leading authority whose book inspired the P-E claim, is portrayed in Jeffrey's book, FINAL WARNING, as "perhaps the most authoritative scholar on the writings of the

[65] http://www.bibleprophesy.org/ancient.htm

early Byzantine Church." But this misleading statement, designed to make readers think that Professor Alexander supports the P-E claim, covers up the fact that this world famous scholar sees not even a smidgen of pretrib in the same Medieval writer!

"In fact, Alexander writes that the phrase "taken to the Lord" (which has become a bonanza for pretrib history revisionists) means "participate at least in some measure in beatitude." While Jeffrey and Ice do include this "beatitude" phrase, all P-E promoters carefully avoid revealing that the Catholic doctrine of "beatitude," according to the NEW CATHOLIC ENCYCLOPEDIA, has to do with "the highest acts of virtue that can be performed in this life" - works on earth and not being raptured off earth! (Elsewhere in his sermon P-E repeats the importance of doing "penance," because of "our sins," so that church members will be "sustained" during the tribulation!)

"In fact (again), Alexander has two summaries (textual and outline), in chronological order, of P-E's endtime events. And guess what. Alexander demonstrates both times that P-E saw only one future coming ("Second Coming of Christ" for the "punishment of the Antichrist") which follows (!) the great tribulation ("lasting three and a half years") - claim-smashing summaries that self-serving promoters, with malice aforethought, have jointly swept under their "secret rapture" rug!"[66]

Why should Dr. Alexander's opinion on the subject be the *final* opinion, with a "case closed" mentality? MacPherson himself would likely *not* put up with that, if the tables were turned and there was one "expert" who disagreed with *him*, would he? Certainly not, yet he expects all to read that and respond with something akin to, *"Well, I guess that settles that question!"*

---

[66] http://www.tribwatch.com/davemac.htm

No, *it does not settle the question.* First, we do not know the exact date of the Pseudo-Ephraem document, and MacPherson admits as much. Secondly, there is *no direct* connection between the Pseudo-Ephraem document and Roman Catholicism at all. While some may see an inference, an inference does not translate to *factual evidence.* One only needs to peruse the many documents and commentary written on the Pseudo-Ephraem document to determine that Dr. Paul Alexander is one "expert" voice among many. Ultimately, a decision to accept, or reject arguments is often normally based upon the individual reader's own positional stance.

As far as this author can determine, the one who evidences "malice aforethought" is Dave MacPherson, along with his followers. The reality is that *MacPherson has proved nothing,* except to those who insist that he is correct. In so doing, they have simply received his information *as if it is the truth,* when in fact a careful reading of his books and articles proves *nothing.* He *resolutely promotes* his own view – Posttribulationalism – and because that is the only view he finds viable, then all others (but especially the PreTrib Rapture), are wrong. Since to him, the PreTrib Rapture position seems untenable, he has set his sights on that doctrinal position, to the exclusion of all others.

Once he feels he has obliterated any attempts by "pretrib promoters," to negate his argument, MacPherson, quickly jumps to Section 10 of this same document, which states:

> "And when the three and a half years have been completed, the
> time of the Antichrist, through which he will have seduced the
> world, after the resurrection of the two prophets, in the hour
> which the world does not know, and on the day which the enemy
> of son of perdition does not know, will come the sign of the Son of
> Man, and coming forward the Lord shall appear with great pow-
> er and much majesty, with the sign of the wood of salvation
> going before him, and also even with all the powers of the hea-

vens with the whole chorus of the saints, with those who bear the sign of the holy cross upon their shoulders, as the angelic trumpet precedes him, which shall sound and declare: Arise, O sleeping ones, arise, meet Christ, because his hour of judgment has come! Then Christ shall come and the enemy shall be thrown into confusion, and the Lord shall destroy him by the spirit of his mouth. And he shall be bound and shall be plunged into the abyss of everlasting fire alive with his father Satan; and all people, who do his wishes, shall perish with him forever; but the righteous ones shall inherit everlasting life with the Lord forever and ever."[67]

So confident is he of his understanding of the Pseudo-Ephraem document, that he makes this sarcastic remark, followed by a question:

> *"In the before-the-tribulation sections, P-E mentions neither a descent of Christ, nor a shout, nor an angelic voice, nor a trumpet of God, nor a resurrection, nor the dead in Christ, nor a rapture, nor meeting Christ."*

If we want to be legalistic, then MacPherson is correct, in that the writer of the document does not refer to a *physical* descent of Christ, a shout, an angelic voice, or a trumpet sound. While he cannot be accused of lying, he can certainly be accused of *revisionism*, since he ignores the *verbiage* of the writer, and the *intended* meaning.

But consider section 2 again; "**For all the saints and elect of God are gathered, prior to the tribulation that is to come, and are taken to the Lord lest they see the confusion that is to overwhelm the world because of our sins**." This should be plain to MacPherson that the writer fully expected the saints and elect to:

- *Be gathered prior to the Tribulation*

---

[67] http://www.bibleprophesy.org/ancient.htm

- *Be taken to the Lord*

The only question that can be asked if we disregard the writer's intended meaning, is *What ELSE could the writer have been referring to, if not a PreTrib Rapture?!* Alexander's interpretation of, and connection to, Roman Catholicism seems strained, since there is no direct internal evidence connecting the document with Roman Catholicism. Regarding this section, MacPherson then asks the question, *"So where does P-E place the rapture?* [68] In spite of the fact that the writer of the document clearly places the Rapture *before* the Tribulation, MacPherson answers his own question thusly;

> *"The answer is found in his last section (10) where he writes that after "the sign of the Son of Man" when "the Lord shall appear with great power," the "angelic trumpet precedes him, which shall sound and declare: Arise, O sleeping ones, arise, meet Christ, because the hour of judgment has come!" (Like Morgan Edwards and Manuel Lacunza, Pseudo-Ephraem has the nasty, non-pretrib habit of blending the rapture with the final advent!) In the July/Sep., 1995 BIBLIOTHECA SACRA, Dallas Seminary's journal, Thomas Ice and his co-author Timothy Demy pulled off one of the worst revisionisms of P-E ever: when summarizing Section 10 they carefully deleted what P-E included between "trumpet" and "judgment" (deleted the distinctive I Thess. 4 aspects in that posttrib setting), giving unsuspecting readers this utterly misleading condensation: "A trumpet will sound, calling forth the dead to judgment." But P-E says much more, as can be seen;* **he places the resurrection of those who sleep in Jesus and the rapture of those who meet Jesus (details found only in I Thess. 4) at the Matt. 24 coming!"**[69] (emphasis added)

---

[68] http://www.thewordsofeternallife.com/deceived.html
[69] Ibid

While he is busy accusing Ice and Demy of perpetrating *"one of the worst revisionisms of P-E ever,"* it is actually *MacPherson* who has done that. He completely ignores the writer's statements in section 2, where it clearly states that the the saints and elect will be *gathered* to the Lord *before* the Tribulation. As if that is not enough, he drops all the way down to the 10th section, where the writer of the document is obviously at that point, referring to the events that will occur at the *end* of the Tribulation:

- The angelic trumpet
- The call to arise and meet Christ
- Christ will come and toss His enemy into confusion
- Then Satan will be cast into the bottomless pit

This is the *exact* same scenario as that which is taught by normal Dispensationalism, and PreTrib Rapturists!

MacPherson's article continues, meandering here and there, getting in as many jabs as possible toward Thomas Ice and others. He even takes the time to point out that the school Ice received his doctorate from was sued by Texas, stating,

> *"Since 'Dr.' Thomas Ice is the most rabid pretrib defender who's long promoted the (false) claims for John Darby and, more recently, Edwards and Pseudo-Ephraem, and at the same time covered up or twisted the (true) claims for Margaret Macdonald and the Irvingites, it's fitting to quote the first sentence of a recent news item: "WorldNetDaily reported on March 7 that a Texas district court has ordered the Tyndale Theological Seminary to pay fines totalling $170,000 for issuing 34 theological degrees without receiving approval from the state education agency."*[70]

---

[70] http://www.thewordsofeternallife.com/deceived.html

The same title – *rabid defender* – could also easily be used to reference Dave MacPherson, since all eight of his books are his attempts to disprove the veracity of the PreTrib Rapture position. That aside, the only possible reason that MacPherson would take the time to point that out, is to denigrate Thomas Ice, as someone who did not have a legitimate doctorate. Of course, MacPherson seems to delight in pointing this out, and hoping that Tyndale will be seen as one of those mail order institutions where money is paid, and a degree is granted. This is not the case with Tyndale. This author can attest to the fact that a good deal of time, energy, and research went into obtaining a Masters in Biblical Studies from Tyndale Theological Seminary. The institution has some of the lowest tuition rates around, and even have scholarships for those who find it difficult to afford even those low rates. Tyndale Theological Seminary is *not* in the business of profiting from selling fake degrees, as some have reported, and MacPherson has implied. One can only wonder how low can MacPherson go?

This statement from Tyndale's own website highlights their accountability:

> *"Tyndale Theological Seminary & Biblical Institute is a ministry of HEB Ministries, a recognized non-profit religious corporation chartered by the State of Texas. HEB Ministries has been granted tax-exempt status by the Texas State Comptroller of Public Accounts and by the Internal Revenue Service as a 501(c)(3) organization."*[71]

Beyond that though, one cannot help but wonder if MacPherson ever followed up on the results of this particular case, which started in 1998, and did not culminate until 2007? There are some excellent reasons why Tyndale Theological Seminary did not want to be accredited by the *Association of Theological Schools (ATS)*.

---

[71] http://www.tyndale.edu/accreditation.html

1. "ATS is Protestant, Roman Catholic and Eastern/Greek Orthodox oriented, which places it outside a sound, Biblical theological position. It's 'nominally' Christian at best. Tyndale has mul-
tiple courses and journal articles that detail the errors of many
of these denominations and "churches" that would be conduct-
ing Tyndale's accreditation review (Roman Catholic, Arminian,
liberal, etc.). Check out the Tyndale website, especially the doctrinal statement.

2. Being liberal in orientation and postmodernist in attitude, ATS
accommodates feminist and lesbian/gay views. See ATS's website. If you drill down under the link "Women in Leadership Se-
minars", you will find labyrinth of links to these radical and
perverse groups.

3. ATS uses "globalization" as one of their primary accreditation
criteria. By this they mean that schools should be promoting
"multiculturalism" in the postmodernist sense of the term.

4. Many believe that accreditation by the ATS (dating from the
early 70's) was one of several contributing factors that caused
the theological shift at Dallas Theological Seminary, including
"Progressive Dispensationalism" (which Miles Stanford wrote
about) and more recently, the "Openness View of God".

5. Tyndale's President and Registrar receive salaries far below the
minimum levels set by accreditation agencies. While Tyndale's
leaders believe it's adequate for the seminary's purposes, the
end result would be substantially higher facility costs. In turn,
Tyndale's tuition levels would obviously have to be increased,
thus placing increased financial hardships on students. These
changes in fiscal policy, mandated for accreditation, put many
schools into debt. Tyndale is currently debt free and doesn't
want to change that.

6. Accreditation guarantees nothing. Tyndale's courses will transfer to some other "accredited" seminaries (like Dallas Theological Seminary), but will not transfer to an "accredited" reformed
seminary (like Westminster, with course availability in the Dallas area). Tyndale's courses are more work than comparable
courses at a school that is accredited. As a graduate of an ac-

credited engineering school (BSCE) and business school (MBA), I can vouch for that. One student who is transferring to Tyndale from Southwestern Seminary (which is accredited) says that only 5 of the approximately 70 instructors at Southwestern believe in biblical inspiration in any conservative sense. Accreditation among theological schools is no guarantee of scholarship, sound doctrine, cost/benefit, or transferability of course work."[72]

Did MacPherson *bother* to research this prior to making the comments he made, in which he intentionally or unintentionally implied an underhandedness by Tyndale? On August 31, 2007, the Texas State Supreme court ruled *in favor* of Tyndale Theological Seminary:

"The court ruled 8-0 that the law wrongly restricted the schools' use of the term "seminary." But the court split on the question of whether or not the state could regulate the granting of seminary diplomas, with two justices arguing the state may exercise such oversight.

"The court wrote: "It is one thing for the State to require that English majors in a baccalaureate program take science or math courses, that they be taught by professors with master's degrees from accredited institutions, and that professors have the freedom to teach that the works sometimes attributed to Shakespeare were really written by Edward de Vere, Christopher Marlowe, Francis Bacon, or Queen Elizabeth I. It is quite another for the State to require that a religious institution's baccalaureate-level education in religion include psychology courses, or that preaching or evangelism or missions be taught only by professors with master's degrees instead of practitioners from the field, or that a school's faculty have the freedom to

---

[72] http://withchrist.org/seminary.htm

teach that the Bible was not divinely inspired, contrary to the school's tenets of faith."[73]

So, *who* is revising *what*, by omission, or any other way? While MacPherson's ill will is demonstrated in castigating Thomas Ice[74], and Grant Jeffrey, he further attempts to defame Ice by casting aspersions on Tyndale Theological Seminary, implying that his doctorate was merely handed to him after *paying* for it. Without reading through all of his books and articles, it is impossible to know whether or not MacPherson ever published any updated information with respect to the Tyndale lawsuit. Certainly, in the interest of fair play, and journalistic *integrity*, one would hope that he has done so, however as of this writing, a quick email to Dr. Ice, revealed that MacPherson has never apologized to him directly, and as far as Dr. Ice knows, MacPherson has never issued any type of retraction.

Once a person begins to delve into the accusatory language of those opposed to the PreTrib Rapture, it quickly becomes apparent that there may, in fact, be something underhanded going on. However, it also appears that the underhandedness might be coming from those who stand in opposition to the PreTrib Rapture.

Thomas Ice, in a new article, *John Nelson Darby and the Irvingites*, copyright 2009, highlights the sheer absurdity of MacPherson's charges. Ice comments, *"Irvingite Robert Norton included a handwritten account of Margaret Macdonald's 'prophecy,'[75] which MacPherson says was the fountainhead for Darby's development of the pretribulational rapture doctrine.[76] MacPherson does not say that*

---

[73] http://www.texanonline.net/default.asp?action=article&aid=5302&issue=9/10/2007
[74] As of 07/11/2009, when I spoke with Thomas Ice, he was not aware of any place where Dave MacPherson had apologized for the implications in his mentioning the lawsuit with respect to Tyndale Theological Seminary, nor has he apologized to Ice.
[75] Macdonald's revelation was first published in a book by physician Robert Norton, who later married Margaret, Memoirs of James & George Macdonald, of Port Glasgow, (London: John F. Shaw, 1840), pp. 171–76.
[76] MacPherson, Hoax, pp. 50–57

Macdonald included a clear statement of the pretribulational rapture, but that she 'separated the Rapture from the Second Coming before anyone else did.'[77] According to MacPherson, Darby pilfered this two-stage teaching from Macdonald and then developed it systematically, skillfully passing it off as the fruit of his personal Bible study.

Macdonald's so-called revelation that MacPherson cites to make his case revolves around two key phrases. 'Margaret dramatically separated the sign of the Son of man from the coming of the Son of man,'[78] declares MacPherson, based on her phrase, 'now look out for the sign of the Son of man'.[79] MacPherson argues that 'she equated the sign with the Rapture—a Rapture that would occur before the revealing of Antichrist'.[80]

He bases this on her statement, 'I saw it was just the Lord himself descending from Heaven with a shout, just the glorified man, even Jesus'."[81]

What is truly astounding is that Dave MacPherson is professed to be the quality journalist others allege him to be! Anyone who actually takes the time to read the account of Margaret MacDonald's vision, ends up being confused! Yet, somehow, Dave MacPherson is able to muddle through it, arriving at the conclusions he arrives at. For those unaware, Margaret MacDonald was a young girl of about fifteen, who allegedly had a vision about the End Times. In it, she stated a number of things about the coming of the Lord and the Rapture. This information was supposedly obtained by J. N. Darby, who then wrote about it. Scofield later picked up where Darby led off, and incorporated this "new" belief into his Scofield Bible Study System. The problem of course, is that there has *never* been a direct

---

[77] MacPherson, *Hoax*, p. 121
[78] MacPherson, Hoax, p. 128
[79] MacPherson, Hoax, p. 125
[80] MacPherson, Hoax, p. 129
[81] MacPherson, Hoax, p. 126

or even an indirect link between MacDonald and Darby! Moreover, when MacDonald's narrative is carefully studied, it cannot even be dogmatically determined that she was referring to a *PreTrib Rapture*!! Why should facts like these stand in the way of those who are simply trying to criticize someone, or their beliefs?

There is a good likelihood that MacDonald was not even thinking of a supposed two-stage coming of the Lord. *"MacPherson has misinterpreted Macdonald's words by equating her use of 'sign' with a rapture. Rather, she is saying that only those who are spiritual will see the secret sign of the Son of Man that will precede the single, posttribulational second coming of Christ. In other words only those who have the light of the Holy Spirit within them will know when the Second Coming will take place because this spiritual enlightenment will enable them to have the spiritual perception to see the secret sign (not the secret rapture).*[82]

In fact, MacDonald mentions Stephen (from the book of Acts), who looked up into the heavens, and saw Christ standing. No one else around him saw this vision, that captivated him. Her point seems to clearly be that *only* those with *spiritual eyesight* will see the Coming of the Lord, as Ice points out. How does one get a *two-stage* Second Coming from this? Only in MacPherson's overactive imagination.

Ice then points out that a number of Posttribulational and Preterist theologians agree that MacDonald was *not* teaching a two-stage Second Coming of Jesus, but was commenting only on the fact that His coming will be seen with *spiritual eyes*.[83]

---

[82] Thomas Ice, *John Nelson Darby and the Irvingites* (article, © 2009)

[83] D. H. Kromminga, The Millennium in the Church: Studies in the History of Christian Chiliasm (Grand Rapids: Wm. B. Eerdmans Publishing Co., 1945), p. 250, and John L. Bray, The Origin of the Pre-Tribulation Rapture Teaching (Lakeland, Fl.: John L. Bray Ministry, n.d.), pp. 21-22. Interestingly Bray argues that Emmanuel Lacunza, a Jesuit priest from Chile, writing under the assumed name of Rabbi Juan Josafat Ben-Ezra as a

Ice brings out another very important point, regarding MacDonald's own theology. He states that, "...*it is highly questionable, as already noted, that Macdonald was referring to the rapture, as MacPherson insists. Also Macdonald was still a **historicist; she believed the church was already in the tribulation and had been for hundreds of years**. Therefore the Antichrist was to be soon revealed, but before the second coming. She said believers need spiritual sight so they will not be deceived.*"[84] (emphasis added)

It becomes exceedingly clear that Margaret MacDonald was a *Posttribulationalist*, as Ice observes, and, in this author's opinion, proves beyond doubt. Some though, refuse to accept or see the truth, in spite of the fact that it stares at them directly in the face. Such seems to be the case with MacPherson, and those who look to *him* for their truth.

Walvoord, Ryrie and others have pointed this out as well. The trouble seems not to be in what Margaret MacDonald *said*, but rather in what some simply *prefer to believe*. What I have noticed about people like MacPherson (and Fisher, as well as Warner and others), is that they seem to believe that by providing a good deal of *peripheral* information, not directly tied to MacDonald's vision, the sheer amount of information they provide, will be enough to convince anyone that what they are presenting is the truth. The trouble with this, is that it is futile at best, because all it serves to do is further muddy the waters, covering over any actual facts they present which are directly related to MacDonald, her vision, or Darby. Their subterfuge serves no purpose, except to expose their own claims as fallacious.

---

converted Jew, came up with a two-staged coming in the 1790s (footnote from Ice's article)

[84] Thomas Ice, *John Nelson Darby and the Irvingites* (article, © 2009)

Ice lists commentator after commentator, historian after historian, who resolutely disagree with MacPherson's own conclusions. Rather than look at the facts, recognize them for what they are, it has become fodder for the rumor mills to believe instead that Darby was a tyrant, filled with ego, and carnal. This character assasination serves their point well; that if he was of such low moral character, then for him to steal what a young girl saw in some supposed vision, would not be beneath him.

The truth of the matter is pointedtly made by Brethren researcher Roy A. Huebner, who alleges that MacPherson's research and results are little more than slanderous statements made about Darby. In spite of this, MacPherson and his followers, continually point out how Darby's alleged tyranny led to all manner of treachery, including, but not limited to, the excommunication of George Müller. Certainly, this act would be tragic, and moreso for anyone who knows the good that Müller accomplished in the Name of God, and by faith in Him.

Without diminishing Darby's responsibility in the matter, it should be noted that *everyone* that has been used of God in some way throughout history, has some *flaw* of character, coupled with *sin*. We see this since time immemorial. For instance, some of the individuals best known for their role in the Reformation had questionable beliefs, to say the least.

Martin Luther, who finally came to the understanding that salvation was a free gift, unmerited by anything that man could do, came to embrace anti-Semitism later on in life that would not go away. In his treastise, *On the Jews and Their Lies*, he wrote in 1543, his hateful attitude toward Jews was clearly evidenced.[85] Some historians note that it was quite possibly this work of Luther's, which ultimately gave

---

[85] http://www.humanitas-international.org/showcase/chronography/documents/luther-jews.htm

rise to the Holocaust, because it was a work that Hitler read nearly every night before retiring.

It is clearly understood that all involved with making the Reformation happen, denying the superiority of the Roman Catholic Church, and its multitude of error, did so under God's direction. Yet not all of the error promulgated by the Roman Catholic Church was dealt with by the Reformers.

Chapter 8
Unprepared?

We have already seen how some individuals make numerous claims regarding what they consider to be the *fallout* of believing the PreTrib Rapture position. Of course, it is understood in almost in all cases, that the people who make the most noise about this are Posttribulationalists.

These folks are convinced that the early Church was Posttribulational in belief, and there was absolutely *no* sign of PreTrib Rapturism to be found anywhere on the landscape of the early Church's horizon.

It would seem that even holding a Posttribulational Rapture does not guarantee a spiritual maturity in Christ. The evidence is simply too obvious. Nevertheless, if the Corinthian church is not enough, what about other epistles that Paul wrote? Do they contain information about specific churches, which highlight an immaturity within Christians that mitigates any claims that a PreTrib Rapture position is the *only* position that creates "ingrown Christians?"

Actually, if we go to the early chapters of Revelation, we see how Jesus Himself viewed these churches. Almost all of those churches had difficulties that put them in danger. Starting in chapter two, we read of seven churches, to which Christ made statements.

1. **Ephesus**
    a. Steadfast in service
    b. Did not tolerate evil
    c. Persisted in good works, did not grow weary
    d. *Left their first love*
2. **Smyrna**
    a. Faithful
3. **Pergamum**
    a. Clung to Christ; not denied Him
    b. Entertained *heresy* of the Nicolaitans
4. **Thyatria**
    a. Good works
    b. Tolerate the *heretical* teachings of "Jezebel"
5. **Sardis**
    a. Spiritually *dead*; need to wake up!
6. **Philadelphia**
    a. Steadfast in faith
7. **Laodicea**
    a. Lukewarm – will be *spit* out of Christ's mouth

The above is a very brief outline of the churches in Revelation. Besides these, we know that Paul wrote letters to Galatians, Ephesians, Colossians, and Philippian Churches, who all had some type of difficulty.

Galatia

We know that the Galatians were quickly leaving he faith! They were being led away by the belief that being a Christian was fine, but an adherence to the principles of Judaism was also necessary. In other words, salvation, though by grace alone, by faith alone, in Christ alone, was being *added to* by men Paul referred to as Judaizers. These men were causing the new believers in the Galatian churches to question their salvation, and start to fall away.

Ephesus

The problem for the Ephesians was that they were tending to become lackadaisical, spiritually self-satisfied. Because they had many blessings in Christ, the temptation was that they did not need to press on. This ultimately, would be their downfall and Paul wanted them to be aware of that, in order to avoid it.

Philippi

Paul wrote to these believers to encourage their perseverance as believers. He provided the example of Christ, as the One who humbled Himself, even to death. How much more should we, as believers? Paul also warns them against legalism and lawlessness, two things that would shipwreck their faith with certainty and swiftness.

Colossae

Paul writes to these believers to counter some of the prevalent beliefs at the time, which insisted that Christ had not really come in the flesh. Belief in this would pull them away from the truth that Christ was/is fully God as well as fully Man.

In these and other epistles, Paul deals with difficulties that each of the churches were facing. These difficulties were endangering the spiritual life of the individual churches and left untreated would, like a cancer, infect the entire Body.

The "Strength" of Posttribulationalism?

In none of the above situations, was the subject of *Eschatology* broached by Paul. Interestingly enough though, since it is insisted that the early Church was Posttribulational in position, one then wonders how and why these believers, being so close to the life of Christ, could have been swayed as they were, to adopting positions which would have easily shipwrecked their faith?

Many Posttribulationalists believe that the PreTrib Rapture position creates spiritually weak and immature Christians, unprepared for persecution. Yet, it is clear from even a cursory read-through of the New Testament that persecution *did* exist during that day and age, as well as weak-kneed, spiritually inept Christians (just read Corinthians). Persecution was obviously gaining momentum, with constant warnings from Paul and other apostles, to stand firm, to live a life that pleases God, to be consistent in their walk of faith.

In spite of the warnings of Paul though, a number of these churches were in the position of nearly stumbling so that they almost completely fell. Their impending failure had *nothing* to do with their view of the End Times, and *everything* to do with a number of other things, that they were being tempted to embrace.

If I decide to stop reading the Bible, no longer give myself to prayer, and begin giving into the temptation that I am peppered with throughout the day, I will become an *ineffective*, spiritually *weak*, *unprepared* Christian.

The only thing that influences Christian life and character is how much time we spend with Him:

- *In prayer,*
- *In the study of His Word, and*
- *In drawing on His strength to overcome the evil that is in the world*

Eschatology really plays no role in the above. A real relationship with Jesus Christ is predicated upon the salvation that He has provided, and we have received. From here on out, it is a continued relationship with Him, and a growing desire to please Him in all areas of life.

This is the walk of the Christian. This is Christianity, practically speaking. This is where the rubber meets the road.

If absolutely nothing is known about the End Times, the absence of that knowledge should not affect a Christian's walk with Christ. If God revealed to all the details that He has chosen to leave out of His Word, that should not provoke the Christian to self-reliance or pride. A true walk with Christ should be such that through each day, I grow closer to Him, because of spending more time with Him in His Word and in prayer.

Whether I happen to believe the Rapture will occur prior to the Tribulation or not, has no bearing on my walk with Christ. It may be another 100, or 1,000 years before the Tribulation begins, and I will long be gone anyway! I could be called home tomorrow, and so could *you*.

What our walk with Jesus entails now is all-dependent upon how we spend our time with Christ. Getting to know Him, submitting daily to His will, seeking to turn from every temptation that seeks to bind us and thanking Him in all things, is what creates within me, the desire, the spiritual growth and ultimately, a life that brings Him glory.

To blame a carnal attitude, or a lack of spirituality on the belief in the PreTrib Rapture, ignores the real problem. Genuine spirituality is such that causes the believer to be consistent. It helps the believer to see and understand that there is nothing better than submitting to Christ, in order that His will be lived in and through us.

Chapter 9
Hitting the Delete Button

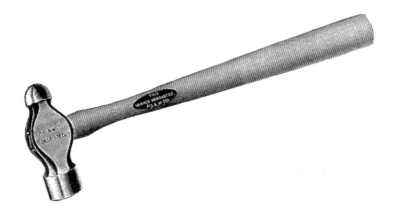

There is a very large problem with all of the books and articles that have come out in an attempt to literally *delete* the PreTrib Rapture doctrine from the face of the church's landscape. After all, how is it that we know all the complaints and charges against the PreTrib Rapture position contain little to no substance? Quite simply, it is because the PreTrib Rapture doctrine is the *only* view of the End Times that has come under serious and constant fire from those opposed to it.

In other words, though proponents of Midtrib, PreWrath and Posttrib Rapture positions stand against one another, they seem to reserve their most heated and vociferous complaints and allegations for the PreTrib Rapture position. This they say is largely due to what they believe to be a heretical position. However, if *one* of the views believed to be incorrect is heretical, then *all* the incorrect views must also be heretical. Yet, such does not seem to be the case when it comes to opposing all positions other than the Pre-Trib Rapture.

We have seen that the various problems individuals have with the PreTrib Rapture doctrine, are due to the following charges:

1. *It's a "new" doctrine, therefore it cannot be correct*
2. *It was derived from people who were seen as being less than authentically Christian*
3. *Apparently, those who believe and espouse the PreTrib Rapture doctrine are mean-spirited, caustic, and will do whatever it takes to silence all those in opposition*
4. *It is deceptive and it is likely part of what Paul speaks of as the "great falling away" of the last days*
5. *It is somehow connected to the "false" Unconditional Eternal Security of the believer*
6. *Those who promoted it were far less educated than the average theologian today, apparently*
7. *Gloom and doom is a great way to scare people into handing over their money!*
8. *It promotes spiritual immaturity and laziness; antino-mianism*

There are other reasons presented, to be sure, however, probably the one that is most telling is reason number **eight**; it supposedly promotes spiritual immaturity and laziness; otherwise known as *antinomianism*. Nevertheless, just because someone *misappropriates* a biblical doctrine, understanding it to mean something it does *not* mean, does not negate the biblical doctrine itself. Yet, this is what we are to believe, claimed by those who oppose the PreTrib Rapture.

If salvation is completely *free*, there is absolutely *nothing* that can be done to earn it. If, however, someone comes along, and *abuses* the understanding of that doctrine, by living a life that is diametrically opposed to one that God expects him to live, this does not make the doctrine of salvation, as revealed in Scripture, null and void. What it means is that someone has attempted to take *advantage* of God's goodness (as if that could really happen), by *telling* themselves that they are saved, yet they continue to live a life that *displeases* God.

However, *none* of these reasons provide us with any type of basis as to why *other* End Times doctrines are not just as vociferously denied. What about Preterism, Replacement Theology, or even the modern-day Emergent Church movement, or Arminianism? A number of theological systems today do not believe in a rapture at all, or in a literal tribulation period, or a literal millennial reign of Christ. These belief systems are filled with what this author believes to be erroneous information concerning the End Times, yet it would appear that taking Dave MacPherson's cue, folks have gathered themselves together, and set their sights upon the PreTrib Rapture doctrine, as if it was the worst thing to come along since the onset of cancer.

The most pointed rebuke to those who insist that the PreTrib Rapture position causes spiritual immaturity and unpreparedness is the fact that, when rightly viewed, the PreTrib Rapture doctrine is nothing different than realizing that each day may very well be the last. Natural death may occur at *any moment*, not only for each Christian, but also for each individual. Should we, as Christians, not be concerned with what may very well be our last day on earth? There is nothing more imminent than death.

Death hangs over the shoulder of every living creature. It is our constant shadow and will affect each of us, except those who are translated from earth to heaven without experiencing death. No one can count on the Rapture to occur during any particular lifetime; however, we can *all* count on the fact that death is a surety.

Dave MacPherson and others are busy arguing that the PreTrib Rapture is a huge cover-up, foisted upon evangelicalism by unsavory individuals. He should probably be spending his time helping people to understand that life is short, and no one knows the day, or the hour when the Lord will have predetermined that each individual will die.

For all the arguing, posturing, debating, writing, castigating, and the like, one cannot help but wonder whether all of this fills MacPherson's wallet, as much as he accuses the PreTrib Rapturist of filling his own. How about it, all of you folks who are so convinced that the PreTrib Rapture is merely a con?

Currently, the End Times is a much-discussed topic. There are many reasons for this, and while discussion of it can be valuable, it can also be counter-productive.

Christ gave us the Great Commission as our marching orders. In it, He tells us,

> "All authority in heaven and on earth has been given to me. Therefore go and make disciples of all nations, baptizing them in the name of the Father and the Son and the Holy Spirit, teaching them to obey everything I have commanded you. And remember, I am with you always, to the end of the age," (Matthew 28:18-20 NET).

The Great Commission tells us to *preach the gospel* about Jesus Christ and the salvation that He came to make available. We are to witness *to* the world, evangelizing them in the Name of the Father, Son and Holy Spirit. The best and most effective way to do this is by living a life that shares the gospel, in word, deed and life in general.

The Great Commission was *never* rescinded. We are *still* obligated (and should *want*), to preach the Good News of Christ's death and resurrection on our behalf. If our entire life revolves around Eschatology – studying it, preaching it, discussing, and/or arguing about it – we are, or will become, a Christian who is out of balance.

I do not believe, for one moment that adopting or espousing a Pre-Trib Rapture position will condemn anyone to hell. As much as I repudiate Preterism and other Eschatological viewpoints allegedly based on Scripture, holding the incorrect view within the realm of Eschatology does not condemn anyone to hell. It is only the *lack of salvation,* which accomplishes that.

Our emphasis in life should be concerned with souls of those who do not know Jesus Christ as Savior. We should not be spending our time attempting to prove this point, or that point within Eschatology. Unless it drives us to action to preach the Word in life, word and deed, to the lost, this is an ineffective use of our time. It is worthwhile to study and appreciate the End Times, if for no other reason than to become much more familiar with the Old Testament! We should gain a greater perspective of God's eternal plans for man throughout history, to the coming eternal order. The Old Testament should not be set aside as the "old" covenant, but as an integral part of God's eternal plans and purposes.

All the debate and discussion related to Eschatology changes nothing. Those who feel it their duty to spend every waking moment immersed in the End Times, are doing no good to anyone, much less, glorifying the Lord. If you are more concerned about "winning the debate," of Eschatology, then you are not concerned enough about the salvation of the lost.

It would be to each Christian's best interest to be about the Master's business. The Master's business is the Great Commission, as our starting point.

Here is an incident, which I find not only fascinating, but also such an expression of deep love for God, that it was evident in the way two brothers responded to one another.

Robert Chapman lived from (1803-1902). His life was a simple, consistent testimony of God's salvation, love, and commitment. Born in Helsingor, Denmark, to a family in which his father owned and operated an import-export business, which had become successful. Eventually, due to the Napoleonic Wars, the family, of necessity, went to England, where Robert continued and finished his formal education.

At age 15, he left home to pursue a 5-year apprenticeship in law. Upon completing that, he opened his own law practice. For some unknown reason though, Robert, at the age of 16, began reading the Bible.

At the age of 20, Robert was invited to attend a church service, where James Harington Evans preached on the justification by faith, through the redemption of Jesus Christ. Chapman received Christ, and began to study the Bible with a renewed vigor. So intent was he to keep the Lord's commandments, that he insisted on baptism as soon as possible, and would not be put off, stating, *"I will make haste, and delay not, to keep His commandments."*[86]

He immediately began working among the poor in London, imploring them to receive the Lord's salvation. Over time, he worked with other individuals, like George Müller, of Bristol, whose heart burned with passion to win souls for the Lord.

Chapman eventually moved into a house where he envisioned a place that would allow those who worked tirelessly for the Lord, to rest and recoup. It would be a place where they would be served, and encouraged.

---

[86] http://www.churchinwestland.org/id286.htm

For the next 70 years, Chapman lived there, ministering to the needs of Christian workers who came there for respite. Whether it was shining their shoes, or reading the Bible to them, Chapman did whatever he could to encourage and strengthen.

During these same 70 years, Chapman worked tirelessly, going door to door, witnessing to the lost on behalf of Jesus Christ. If he was not doing that, he could be found in the middle of the town square, preaching the gospel to all who passed by.

Just as George Muller had his associate in the Lord's work, Henry Craik, so too, did Chapman have his. Together, Chapman worked with William Hake for years, endlessly working to bring the gospel to the lost.

Shortly after Hake's death, Chapman looked back on over 50 years of harmonious work for the Lord. He had nothing but compliments for his close friend and co-worker, who had gone on to be with the Lord they had both served.

What is most interesting here, is that,

"Chapman maintained a 'post-tribulational' view of the Rapture of the church, while Hake (and most of their friends) held a different position. But their Christlike love for one another overshadowed all such disagreements.[87]

Though they disagreed over areas of Eschatology, so great was their desire to introduce the lost to salvation in Christ, that they gladly set aside these doctrinal differences, for the greater work of preaching the Gospel of Christ. *"In fact, Chapman would not allow his view on the time of Christ's return to cause division in the church. He demonstrated his humble and submissive spirit by submitting to the other*

---

[87] Robert L. Peterson & Alexander Strauch, *Agape Leadership* (Colorado Springs: Lewis and Roth Publishing 1991), 61

elders on this point of disagreement. In 1896, he called the elders at Bear Street together 'to explain that I shall not create dissension by teaching the opposite view of the assembly.' For the sake of unity, he would not teach against the position of the other elders; yet he saw no need to change his interpretation. Concerning essential doctrines and scriptural principles, however, Chapman remained firm."[88]

This world needs more Christians like Robert Chapman. We need more people who are willing to set differences aside, which are peripheral to the area of salvation, and to work together to introduce the lost to the Lord. We cannot do this if we are arguing over this point or that point, or worse, if we are deciding that we know who will and who will not, be destined for hell, based on a person's particular Eschatological viewpoint. What matters infinitely more than being correct about the End Times is being correct about *salvation*. Not only being correct about it, but preaching it, praying to the Lord of the Harvest that He would open the eyes of those we preach to, in order that they would receive His salvation.

It is the salvation *that only the Lord provides,* which results in spiritual growth and resultant works that please and glorify the Lord! This cannot be stated more strongly. We can spend the remainder of our lives, arguing over things that in the short or long run do not really matter, or we can spend the remainder of our lives, submitting ourselves to His will, fulfilling the Great Commission. In considering the landscape of the visible Church today, it becomes clear, that it is littered with many things that are not intended to bring glory to the Lord. While on one hand, everything will ultimately bring Him glory, it is our responsibility as His children, and His elect, to be generous in passing along the same gospel message that came to us, and bears fruit.

---

[88] Robert L. Peterson & Alexander Strauch, *Agape Leadership* (Colorado Springs: Lewis and Roth Publishing 1991), 61

Let us put everything that serves to distract from God's purposes aside, that we may preach Him crucified, and who rose on the third day from the grave. He has forever been victorious over Satan, sin and death. It is in Him that we also gain that same victory. We *must* endeavor to live the life that pleases Him.

Realizing that Jesus is going to return one day, is in and of itself, uplifting. It purifies the soul, by allowing us to see immediately the importance (or lack thereof), of any circumstance we find in our lives.

To do nothing but stare up into the heavens, as the disciples did immediately after Christ's ascension, does absolutely *nothing* to further His work, or His kingdom. While studying and discussing the End Times is a worthwhile pursuit, it is *not* going to grant salvation to any individual (nor will it cast anyone into hell). Studying the End Times, is not a *primary* concern, and should not be treated as such.

Salvation is *the* primary concern and it is here that we find ourselves on the same road that Jesus Himself. We must be willing to forget ourselves, as Christ "forgot" Himself, in order that we might have life. We must let go of our lives, in order that Christ might live His eternal life in and through us.

There is no other way to bring glory to God, and the Church needs to wake up to that fact. It is the preaching of the cross to the lost. It is bringing the gospel of Christ to those who are perishing. It is for this reason that Christ came and it is for this reason, that He leaves us here after we receive His salvation.

No one will live forever on this planet, without ever seeing death (aside from those who are alive to enter the Millennial Kingdom). Have you – *do you* – consider the fact that each day on this planet could be *your* last? God could call any one of us, home at any moment.

Are we living each day as if God *will* call us home sometime during that 24-hour period? If not, we most definitely *should*. Forget the Rapture. Death *may* take us long before that ever happens. May we spend the remainder of our days, bringing Him glory, by bringing him lost soul, after lost soul.

NOTES

Resources for Your Library:

BOOKS:

- Basis of the Premillennial Faith, The, by Charles C. Ryrie
- Biblical Hermeneutics, by Milton S. Terry
- Daniel, the Key to Prophetic Revelation by John F. Walvoord
- Dictionary of Premillennial Theology, Mal Couch, Editor
- Daniel, by H. A. Ironside
- Daniel: The Kingdom of the Lord, by Charles Lee Feinberg
- Daniel's Prophecy of the 70 Weeks, by Alva J. McClain
- Exploring the Future, by John Phillips
- Footsteps of the Messiah, by Arnold G. Fruchtenbaum
- For Zion's Sake: Christian Zionism and the Role of John Nelson Darby, by Paul Richard Wilkinson
- Future Israel (Why Christian Anti-Judaism Must Be Challenged), by E. Ray Clendenen, Ed.
- God's Plan for Israel, Steven A. Kreloff
- Israel in the Plan of God, by David Baron
- Israelology, by Arnold G. Fruchtenbaum
- Moody Handbook of Theology, The by Paul Enns
- Most High God (Daniel), by Renald E. Showers
- Mountains of Israel, The, by Norma Archbold
- Pre-Wrath Rapture Answered, The, by Lee W. Brainard
- Prophecy 20/20 by Dr. Chuck Missler
- There Really Is a Difference! by Renald Showers
- Things to Come, by J. Dwight Pentecost
- What on Earth is God Doing? By Renald Showers

Order Other Books by Fred DeRuvo

From the following places:
www.studygrowknow.com • www.amazon.com
www.prophecyinthenews.com • www.createspace.com

5482800R0

Made in the USA
Charleston, SC
21 June 2010